LIFE'S
TOO
SHORT
TO MISS
THE BIG PICTURE

STEVE DIGGS

LIFE'S TOO SHORT

TO MISS
THE BIG PICTURE

Making the Most
of What's Most Important

LEAFWOOD
PUBLISHERS

Abilene, Texas

Unless otherwise noted, Scripture quotations are taken from the NEW AMERICAN STANDARD BIBLE®, copyright © 1960, 1962, 1963, 1968, 1971, 1972, 1973, 1975, 1977, 1995 by The Lockman Foundation. Used by permission. www.Lockman.org. Scripture quotations marked GNT are taken from the GOOD NEWS TRANSLATION, SECOND EDITION. Copyright © 1992 by American Bible Society. Used by permission. All rights reserved. Scripture quotations marked KJV are taken from The Holy Bible, King James Version. Scripture quotations marked MSG are taken from THE MESSAGE. Copyright © 1993, 1994, 1995, 1996, 2000, 2001, 2002. Used by permission of NavPress Publishing Group. Scripture quotations marked NIV are taken from the HOLY BIBLE, NEW INTERNATIONAL VERSION ®. Copyright © 1973, 1978, 1984 by International Bible Society. Used by permission of Zondervan Publishing House. All rights reserved. Where indicated, scripture quotations are taken from the Holy Bible, New Living Translation, copyright © 1996. Used by permission of Tyndale House Publishers, Inc., Wheaton, Illinois 60189. All rights reserved.

Cover design by Stephanie Walker
Interior text design by Sandy Armstrong

LIBRARY OF CONGRESS CATALOGING-IN-PUBLICATION DATA
Diggs, Steve.
Life's too short to miss the big picture : making the most of what's most important / Steve Diggs.
    p. cm.
ISBN 978-0-89112-640-9
1. Christian life. I. Title.
BV4501.3.D55 2010
248.4--dc22

2010008087

Leafwood Publishers, 1626 Campus Court, Abilene, Texas 79601
1-877-816-4455 toll free

For current information about all Leafwood titles, visit our Web site:
www.leafwoodpublishers.com

10 11 12 13 14 15 / 7 6 5 4 3 2 1

To our son, Josh—a true man of God
who is everything I want to be when I grow up.

Acknowledgements

Like any project of this sort, this book didn't happen in a vacuum. The life skills I share were learned from a host of people. Although neither is still here to read this book, my parents' fingerprints are all over it. They were my first and most important mentors. Following their foundational influence came many others: Rubel Shelly, Batsell Barrett Baxter, Alton Howard, and on and on. But special thanks for this project must go to three wonderful and most patient men: Bucky Rosenbaum represents me as a writer and encouraged me to accept this assignment. Denny Boltinghouse is an old friend and a most patient editor. And special thanks to Leonard Allen who has guided, advised, and helped sharpen the concepts within these pages.

CONTENTS

INTRODUCTION

I sometimes feel like the kid in the MilkBone pajamas—living in a dog-eat-dog world.

When Gary Myers, of Leafwood Publishers, asked me to write this book I was honored, but I almost passed. The deadline was short and my schedule was packed. In addition to my day job as a Christian life-skills speaker (presently that docket is loaded with scores of commitments), I was still working on two other books as well as a weekly newspaper column and a regular TV segment. Sure, God could flood the earth in forty days and Jesus could fast for forty days—but could I do this book justice in just a few months?

For most of a week I vacillated from believing it was doable, to being terrified to even try. I prayed, but God seemed silent. It wasn't until 7:45 during a Wednesday evening Bible class (sometimes my mind wanders) that it hit me: I could not *not* write this book! Within twenty minutes, I had called and accepted the opportunity.

However, by the next day, those doubts were closing in again. "What will I say?" And more importantly, "What *right* do I have to say these things anyway?" The very things that I write about in this book have often mowed my own toes off at the ankles. Besides, this book has been a dream of Gary's for years. I didn't want to let him down. I wanted to give the most book for the bang possible.

Thankfully, God settled my mind as I reread Gary's vision for this volume: *"I have always felt a kindred spirit with David because like him I have been fighting Goliaths all my life. This is not to say I have been overwhelmingly victorious. On the contrary, my Goliaths have beat me down, humiliated me, left me bruised and bloody, fired me and done overall damage to heart, soul, and mind . . . . If there is any sadness attached to this book it is that most of us go through life and discover the truth of it when life's richest moments are already over.... This book is for you if you are discouraged, distressed, dislodged, defeated, or disenfranchised."*

Since that night, my focus has sharpened, and so has my resolve. I needed to write this book for *me*. Here I am, teaching other people the life-skills and the God-skills that are necessary to get it right before we're toe-tagged and horizontal—but it has been a long time since I have fed my own soul.

Maybe you can identify with what happens to many of us when we run out of answers before we run out of questions. This is when we realize that we're not experiencing the "peace that passes understanding" that we had once expected. And gradually we resign ourselves to what one writer has called a "sin management lifestyle." We sort of make an uneasy pact: "Okay, I won't commit the 'biggees.' I won't murder or rob the convenience store. But I'm not going to worry about the broken relationships in my life, or the lies I tell, or the greed, or the pride, or the worry, or the divisive spirit, or that nagging doubt about my walk with Jesus. I'll fake it until I make it."

If you identify with this, we are fellow strugglers, you and I. Let me invite you to peek over the backyard fence and watch as I attempt to clean up my own backyard. Some of this stuff is going to force me to rethink how I'm doing life. I have the sense that you, too, will find some real life answers in these pages. So feel free to get your ticket punched and join me on this ride.

After all, if God could speak through a donkey in the Old Testament, maybe he can use me to make the case that life is too short, and our relationships are too dear, to miss the big picture.

1

SEE THE BIG PICTURE—ONE SMALL CHANGE AT A TIME

The spring of 1974 was a bummer. I was about to graduate from a small Christian college in Nashville—with mediocre grades and even less exciting prospects for the future. There was a local bookstore that had offered me a job. But in the grand scheme of things that seemed slightly less exciting than watching a refrigerator bulb burn out. Then there was the college. They had interviewed me for a job in the recruiting department. (Ironically the salary they were offering did not help me make the case that the school produced graduates with the ability to earn a living wage.) But that job fell through when the collective wisdom of the school's hierarchy determined that I wasn't the proper poster child to promote the Christian mission of the school. Maybe it had something to do with my long hair.

So, as I mentioned, I wasn't sure what lay ahead of me when I received the sheepskin and stepped off the platform. Fortunately, Dave Floyd suggested that we talk. Dave was a friend from church who lived in a beautiful home and ran a successful real estate firm. One evening he asked, "Steve, have you ever considered a career in real estate?"

Well, yes. But other equally enthralling matters had crossed my mind too—like becoming the proprietor of a condemned ferris wheel! In short, I didn't want to spend my life selling stuff to people who didn't want it. But, short of other viable options, I said, "Sure!"

Fortunately, Dave took me under his wing and taught me a lot. Knowing that I didn't want to be a high pressure sales guy, he used an analogy that has served me well through the years. Here, with some adaptation from me, is what Dave said. "Steve, selling is like taking someone for a swim. Even if you own the most inviting pool in town, not everyone will want to take a dip. Your job is not to hide in the bushes and grab unsuspecting people and bodily throw them into the pool fully clothed. Instead, your job is to look for people who seem to have the time, temperament, and interest to take a swim. Then, when you meet such a person, ask politely, 'May I show you my new swimming pool?' If the person agrees, lead him over and invite him to look around at his leisure. If he seems interested, suggest that he put his toe into the cool water. Point out that, since he's free for the afternoon, and since it's so warm, a dip in the pool would be great fun. Then, assuming he's interested, you might mention, 'There are some swim suits in the changing room, feel free to put one on.' Then, if he accepts your offer, put a swim suit on yourself, walk to the pool together, and gently tap him on the shoulder, and say, 'Why don't we jump in together?'"

That day Dave taught me an important lesson. The best way to make vital life changes involves three things:

1. A coach who is willing to become personally involved.
2. A coach who believes enough in his own advice to follow it himself.
3. A coach who has "been there and done that" and sees the benefit—or the big picture.

My purpose in this book is to help you refocus and see what really matters. Big picture thinking involves learning to instinctively invest our time and energy in what matters rather than in the minutia that depletes many of our lives. I will show you how to major in the majors—so the minors will take care of themselves. Part of this involves the freeing realization that every simple action you take will make a positive difference. Don't think of this as a book that must be fully read, digested, and mastered in order to see significant benefits. You will find some of the chapters most helpful—and doable. Others you may lay aside for later consideration. That's fine. My advice: Make one small change. Enjoy the benefits of that change. Then consider making another.

In this book I will lead you on a journey. You will be reminded of some important life skills that you once knew but over the years have misplaced in the weeds of a hectic life. You will be challenged to rethink some long-held beliefs and blow the dust off of some long-settled "truths." Finally, you will learn some totally fresh, new, bold perspectives that will improve your life trajectory.

I have written this book for people who are sick and tired of being sick and tired. It's for those of you who are beginning to realize that life is too short *not* to get things right. These seventy "life chapters" are for people who are tired of missed opportunities and spiritually disheveled lives. My goal is to encourage you to make the small changes, one after another, that will make it very easy for your family to find six willing pallbearers.

In the process of learning to see God's big picture for your life, everything else will begin to come into focus. You will learn the importance of doing the right thing—simply because it *is* the right thing. You will understand the futility of manipulating life events to suit a personal agenda. And, despite what our present pop culture is selling, you will begin to understand that God is much more than your cosmic bell hop.

We are fellow strugglers, you and I. Both of us have had some wins—and some painful losses. I believe that God wants each of us to lead a spiritually vigorous life. The book you are holding throbs with the strategies, skills, and disciplines needed to clear out the brush and really see the big picture that God has for you. When we begin to see the big picture, priorities also come into focus. We are finally able to make our past the past. We realize that the big picture is all about knowing God, loving family, playing with friends, appreciating life—and jumping into the pool with a friend.

2

VALUE TRADITION

One of the most memorable lines in the tremendously popular musical *Fiddler on the Roof* came from the song sung by Zero Mostel in his role as Tevye. Tevye bellowed out "Tradition!" There is something within most of us that hungers for anchors and an unshakeable bedrock—tradition.

Life is too short not to live it with traditions. Traditions help squeeze the most out of every moment God allows us. At its core, tradition is all about leaving memories for the ones we love and lead.

In the 1950s, dad and mom were like so many other post-war parents. They wanted the best for us—but time and money were always in short supply. But there were some things dad never scrimped on. One of those was the way he did Christmas. Visiting Santa at the store was fine—but not good enough for my dad. So for several Christmas Eves in the mid-1950s there would be a knock on our front door just before bedtime. When we opened the door, there he stood: Santa Claus in all his glory! Now this wasn't some fake, pretend, "my best friend's dad dressed up in a red suit" type Santa. This guy was the real deal.

How did I know? Because he told me so. He probably told us how Rudolf was on the roof with the other reindeer and Mrs. Claus was also wishing us well. Santa explained that, because my sisters and I were so important to him, he simply wanted to take a minute and stop by *our* home before he began his round-the-world flight. Then he would invite us to sit in his lap and remind him of what we wanted. Finally, just before rushing off to begin his journey,

Santa would open his sack and pull out a small gift for each of us. With a last hug, he would bid us a loving goodbye. Then he was gone—leaving three thrilled, wide-eyed youngsters who were determined to obediently hop into bed and go to sleep so he could come back with the rest of our toys.

It was some years later that dad explained to me how he pulled off this feat of tradition building. Dad combined his persuasive skills along with five dollars (not a small amount in those days) to induce the "Santa" at Loveman's department store to stop by our home before he got out of his red suit. Fake? Maybe. Something a more enlightened kid would have figured out? Probably. But for us, knowing how special we were to Santa made Christmas unforgettable.

So, it may come as no surprise when I tell you that, when we began hatching our own kids in the early 1980s, I was determined to do the same thing—sort of. Thanks to dad's inspiration, I wanted to do one better. "How neat would it be," I wondered, "to see my own kids through the eyes of Santa?"

So with the help of my mother, we made it happen. (Mom had grown up hard on a dirt farm in Kentucky. Store-bought cloth was a luxury for her family of ten, so she became quite a seamstress.) Mother designed and tailored the perfect Santa suit for her grown son. This wasn't one of those tacky, cheap red things that looked like oversized pajamas. Oh no. Mother knew how important this mission was. She used the best red velvet and white fur fabric she could find. We bought a real belt with a big metal buckle. And none of those cheap fake boots (that fit over your shoes) for this Santa. We got real, black boots. And for the beard we ordered special, very believable white whiskers that came off an angry yak somewhere. Then, with just enough makeup to supply the "rosy red cheeks" and a pair of rimless eyeglasses, I was ready for my role of a lifetime.

Suffice it to say, from that first Christmas Eve, with only two of what would become four children, Santa at the Diggs' home became an annual tradition. Every Christmas it was the same routine. Dad had to leave for the office shortly after dinner. Then a few minutes later (after a quick wardrobe change) there was a knock at our front door. The children would open the door with huge smiles as Santa did the obligatory, "Ho, ho, ho's!" Then we'd all gather in the living room and get caught up on the previous year's activities—and behavior. Then Santa would open his sack and hand each child the most beautiful orange. Finally, with snapshots taken, the old gentleman would explain that, because "Megan, Joshua, Emilee, and Mary Grace are so important to me, I wanted to stop and visit with you specially before I see all the other children around the world. But now I really must go." So, with a flourish, Santa exited the door he had entered as he called to his team of reindeer on the roof, "Come on Rudolf, and Dancer. . . ."

Shortly, dad would return from the "office" to be met by four children who were at once filled with exciting news, but also saddened that "Daddy missed Santa Claus." Then we would all sit in front of the fireplace and eat our oranges as I read *Twas' the Night Before Christmas*. Finally, we would end the evening by sharing the true story of Christmas from Luke 2, and the children would head for bed.

Now, let me let you in on a little secret: This became tiring after a number of years. Between the rush of Christmas Eve services at church and the other Christmas hubbub, I began to look forward to my retirement as Santa Claus. But I was surprised to learn that our then grown children had no intention of ending this tradition. So, to this day, each Christmas Eve I dutifully don Mother's red velvet suit and see Santa through the eyes of my children.

Some twenty-five years ago, dad went home to be with Jesus. About five years ago mom slipped into his arms, too. But I have a feeling that every Christmas eve, God permitting, they tune in for the tradition.

3

COUNT
YOUR BLESSINGS

At 3:51 this morning I was livid. I had just been awakened from a deep
sleep after a late night arrival at my hotel in Fort Myers. In less than six
hours I was due at a church to preach. And in the room next door, as one old
song phrased it, "There was a party going on." I heard the conversation, the
music, and someone with a set of lungs that could have scuba dived without
the tank! Actually, I'm not sure what it was. What I did know was that it was
the source of unwelcomed noise in the middle of the night.

Finally, I picked up the phone and firmly requested that security come
up and quiet things down. It worked—for about twenty minutes. Then it
started again. By then I was seething. "I paid for this room," I thought. "They
have no right to destroy my good night's sleep." So again I called downstairs.
Again someone came up and sternly required that the havoc cease and desist.

Finally, maybe half an hour later, things seemed to settle down. But it's
what happened during those thirty or so minutes that I want to share with
you. As I lay in my bed with an extra pillow over my head, some thoughts
began to formulate. There was a bigger picture to be seen.

First, I found myself beginning with a comparative analysis. Compared
to many other people around the world at that very moment in time (now
almost five o'clock) I was having a pretty good night. I wasn't lying in bed

awake because we'd just learned that my wife Bonnie has cancer. I wasn't a mother brooding in an emergency room waiting for the doctor to return with news about the seizure my four-year-old had experienced a couple of hours earlier. I wasn't in a warzone playing cards with my buddies (and probably listening to their music) as they kept watch so I could get in my two-hour sleep shift. I wasn't in a refugee camp in a Third World nation with thieves everywhere and an open sewer only feet from my bed roll. No, I was in a nice hotel complete with a flat panel television, a king-sized bed accessorized with plenty of extra pillows, and a great air conditioning system—all adjacent to a bathroom complete with all the amenities, including one of those fancy shower heads. Besides, my sleep wasn't nearly as important as it would have been if I had to get up this morning and lead a squad of soldiers through hostile streets searching for IEDs.

Comparatively speaking, my life was a dream—even if my dreams had been temporarily interrupted. I also began to remember that this is how we grow spiritually: by turning the lemons of spiritual temptation into the lemonade of gratitude. This led me to my second middle-of-the-night spiritual epiphany.

Actually this one was inspired by the words of that great twentieth-century American theologian, Bing Crosby. Do you remember *White Christmas*, the perennially popular movie he starred in? There's a scene in that movie where Bing wanders into the hotel restaurant in the middle of the night and notices that Rosemary Clooney, also unable to sleep, was also there. Bing and Rosemary make a sandwich and pour a glass of milk. As they seat themselves, Bing lets loose with one of his baritone bonanzas as he intones, "If you're worried and you can't sleep, try counting your blessings instead of sheep, and you'll fall asleep counting your blessings." Wow. Thanks, Lord. That's solid theology. So I began counting my blessings. Admittedly, it took a while for me to cool my jets, but guess what? The next thing I knew, the sun was shining.

4

VALUE WHAT
GOD DOES

I don't like to miss introductions. That's why I always try to catch the first few minutes of a television show or a movie. That's why I hate to arrive late to a play. Somehow, if I miss the introduction, I feel uninformed and a bit adrift.

It's sort of the same way with God. When we miss God's introduction, we don't get the big picture. Then we are left without the necessary tools to be about his business. Sadly, most of our postmodern culture is in just such a predicament.

Whatever man was intended to be, it is clear that that is not what he has become. Do you ever find yourself wondering, "Could it be that we Christians are wrong and the secular humanists are right? Maybe life, in fact, has no intrinsic value. Maybe humanity is nothing more than a random alignment of chemicals."

Granted we live in an increasingly crass and coarse culture. Fewer people understand the art of gentility. Disrespect abounds. Human dignity and worth are foreign concepts to many. Far too much value is placed on whether something (or someone) is "useful" to society. And with that as our basic criteria, it becomes increasingly easy to "end a pregnancy" or stop medical aid to the aged—today's equivalent of putting an aging Eskimo on an ice float and pushing him out to sea.

I suspect that much of this problem is the result of humanity having missed *God's Introduction*. God spoke very early and directly about the human condition: "Then God said, 'Let us make man in our image, in our likeness, and let them rule over the fish of the sea and the birds of the air, over the livestock, over all the earth, and over all the creatures that move along the ground'" (Genesis 1:26, NIV).

As Augustine said, there is a "God-shaped vacuum" in our souls. And I believe this short passage in the first chapter of the Bible is at the epicenter of that fundamental truth. It is, in a very real sense, the human genome of the spirit. Until we understand the profound depth and exquisite implications of this simple passage we will never really "get" God's big picture.

Reread the words from the passage slowly and drink them in. Do you see God's symmetry? We are made to be like God. We are not animals. Despite PETA's protests to the contrary, we rule over the animals. We have value because we are human. And humans have value because we are made in the image of our God.

When one comprehends the implications of this, it will prevent us from ever showing disrespect to God by disrespecting anyone made in his image. Profanity and hateful comments are not acceptable because someone "lacks the vocabulary to adequately express himself." No, profanity and hurtful words are wrong because they show disrespect to a fellow human being made in the image of God. Euthanasia cannot be rationalized because *all* humans have value. Why? Simply because they are human. And abortion is not acceptable because it ignores that what you are right now is exactly what that unborn baby will become, if left alone.

You have never seen a mere mortal—because as C. S. Lewis said, "There *are no mere mortals*." All mortals are God-designed and God-formed.

Do you remember that day in Jesus' ministry when some Jewish legalists approached the Teacher trying to trap him with the question: "Tell us then, what is your opinion? Is it right to pay taxes to Caesar or not?" Seeing through their hypocrisy, Jesus zeroed in on the real issue: "'You hypocrites, why are you trying to trap me? Show me the coin used for paying the tax. They brought him a denarius, and he asked them, 'Whose portrait is this? And whose inscription?' 'Caesar's,' they replied. Then he said to them, 'Give to Caesar what is Caesar's, *and to God what is God's.*' When they heard this, they were amazed. So they left him and went away" (Matthew 22, emphasis mine, NIV).

For much of my life I thought that I understood the point of this story. But one thing confused me. I wondered what Jesus meant by giving "to God what is God's?"

I believe maybe I've figured it out in light of the earlier passage from Genesis. Could the ultimate implication be that, since we are all created in the image of God, then the things of God that Jesus spoke of are those of us he made in his image? And if we are "God's things" then doesn't it follow that no one is beyond the reach or the love of God? That is the good news!

5

GET BACK TO BASICS

I f you want to study the Greek and go through those upper level theology courses, that's fine. I've taken some of them myself. But, in truth, I suspect many of us learned most of the theology we really needed to know by the time we were about four years old:

> *Jesus loves me, this I know;*
> *Because the Bible tells me so.*
> *Little ones to Him belong.*
> *We are weak, but He is strong.*

Folks, that is bedrock theology. That's the big picture! Dress it up, tangle it up, or scholarship it up anyway you wish—that's still the thrust of all sixty-six books of the Bible.

I don't care if you're four or 104, we're all still "little ones" in Jesus' economy. We are all broken people and in desperate need of his touch. And the good news is he loves us. I don't know why—but, thank God, he does!

But allow me to put a sharper point on this. Sometimes we hear something (even if it's a good thing) too often. Finally we stop paying attention. It's as though the words go into ear number one, and the grey matter in the middle doesn't even slow them down before they exit by way of ear number two.

So let me say this same thing in a way that will be a little harder for some of us to hear: Jesus *likes* you. I don't care who you are, or where you've been, or what you've done, or who you've done it with. Have you cheated someone this week in a business deal? Did you profane your spouse last night—or break your promise to her? Did you cheat on a test? Did you do something that makes it hard to go to sleep—or to get up in the morning? I repeat, Jesus is still your biggest fan. He may be disappointed in your choices (spelled, s-i-n-s), but he's still pulling for you. He still believes in you. No matter how dark it gets, Jesus is as near as your next breath—and just as vital. As Max Lucado has so succinctly said, if Jesus had a refrigerator in heaven he would have each one of our pictures stuck on the front. *That's* the God we serve!

When they asked Jesus what was required to get right with God, he essentially said, "Are you serious? Do you really want to know? Okay, then buckle your seatbelts and I'll tell you. It takes two things. First, you must learn to love God from your DNA out—with everything that you have and are. That love must be emotional and rational. It must be deep and abiding—and not dependent on always getting what you want. And second, you must learn to love other folk like you already love yourself. This means you will consider their interests. Sometimes it may mean giving another person your place in line—and moving to their place at the rear" (Very loosely paraphrased from Mark 12:29-31).

Jesus had a way of simplifying things for people like you and me who come from the shallow end of the gene pool. He deliberately chose not to come as a philosopher or an intellectual. Yet, for two thousand years we've busied ourselves complicating the simple, confusing the seeking, and piling burdens on others that we don't even carry ourselves. What if I set about to make Jesus more reachable to others? Then maybe he would become more reachable to me.

Big picture thinking means de-cluttering the storage bins of our religious worlds and getting back to the basics.

6

BECOME A
BEAUTIFUL LISTENER

If relations with others mean a lot to you (but sometimes they seem to elude you), you'll find this helpful: become a beautiful listener.

When someone speaks to you, stop and listen—really listen. This little habit will make our all-too-short lives far richer. Try to listen without thinking about what you're going to say next. Avoid "one-ups-manship" listening. This is when I listen to you while thinking of a response that will make whatever you just told me sound less important. The goal as a "one-ups-manship" listener is to "best" you at your own story.

For instance, you step up to me at a party and tell me about how you just found the deal of a lifetime on that Corvette convertible you've always dreamed of, all at half the market value. Then, instead of responding to what you have just said with kudos and "at-a-boys," I feel compelled to tell you about the time I bought a Jaguar (which I've never done) directly from Mario Andretti (whom I've never met) for less than the price of a Chevy Malibu (although I've never met him, I'm certain Mario isn't a fool).

The reason people talk to other people isn't always just to communicate data. It is also to communicate emotion, illicit empathy, and to receive those much needed, "Wows!" When I let my ego drive the conversation, it defeats the purpose of communication—and deflates the person speaking to me.

If you want to be a good listener, there are a few basic things to learn.

First, it's *not* about you. This conversation is about the other person. Allow her to be in the driver's seat. Don't look rushed. Turn your body in that person's direction and add a smile to your face (unless it's really sad news at which time a more somber look might be appropriate.) Maintain good eye contact. (This brings to mind the old proverb, "The eyes are the windows to the soul.") Nod your head affirming that your heart is really *hearing* what the other person is saying.

Second, probe with questions—lots of them. When the person slows down, don't use it as an excuse to turn the conversation to yourself—or to run for the door. Instead, think of the person talking to you as a large, soaked bath towel. Wring that towel for all it's worth. When there's a lull in the conversation, ask another penetrating question like, "So, did you meet Mario personally?" That will achieve exactly what your teller needs. It will encourage further conversation which is the healing balm of human relation.

When you think about it, this is exactly what a good psychiatrist does. (You know, the type who charges $180 an hour.) He listens. Then he asks a question. Then he listens some more. I have a very close friend who went through a bout of depression. I suggested that she visit a psychiatrist for whom I have a lot of respect. Over the months, she told me several times, "I don't understand how he's helping me because he never tells me what to do—he mostly just listens." But somehow that listening, combined with just the right mixture of probing questions, seemed to help. (Of course there was also some medicine and plenty of prayer.) But, thankfully, today this young woman is living a happy, normal life again.

Third, become a public relations expert for the teller. In most cases it's wisest not to repeat the other person's story unless you have a clear sense that it would honor him. Instead, bring the person over to another cluster of friends, and say, "You've got to hear Jeff's story!" Jeff will beam. Others will be enlightened. And you will be Jeff's hero.

Fourth, despite what I said above, it *is* sort of about you. If you become nothing more than a "gimmick listener" you'll only harm yourself and be the worse for it. You will find yourself listening, but not listening. You'll simply be gaming the other person like an animal does its quarry. Become an emotional participant. Learn to live the experiences you listen to vicariously. Learn to "laugh with those who laugh and cry with those who cry." Then, my friend, you will be a part of the family of humanity.

7

DON'T ALLOW VIRTUE TO BECOME VICE

Have you ever stopped to wonder just exactly what the devil has to work with? After all, if we believe that God made the world; and that God made all the stuff in the world; and that all the stuff God made is good stuff—then it begs the question, "What's the devil got to work with?"

The fact is, all the devil has to work with is the good stuff that God has made. He simply takes God's good things and twists them just a little, and perverts them—then he tries to sell them back to us. Sex is a party provided it's within the bond of marriage. But outside of marriage, God's ultimate purpose for the sexual relationship is cheapened. Ambition is a wonderful attribute if we use it to bring out our peak performance. But if we use it as an excuse to claw over other people to selfishly get what we want, then it has become a bad thing.

A healthy interest in our money is right and proper. Christians have every good reason to be interested in how to get it, give it, and grow it. But, if we let our interest in money morph just a little bit, it can become greed. And greed is a killer. It kills both temporally and eternally. King Solomon (arguably the richest guy who ever lived) could have bought and sold Bill Gates twice in a day's time with the change that fell through holes in his tunic. This guy knew his way around money. Here's what he had to say, "Whoever loves money never has money enough; whoever loves wealth is never satisfied with his income" (Ecclesiastes 5:10, *NIV*). Greed leads a lot of God's best and brightest into tremendous sin and bondage. In the South we have an old saying, "The pigs get fat and the hogs get slaughtered."

Big picture thinking has a lot to do with stewardship, a concept that I mention elsewhere in this book. As a follower of The Way, God expects me to redeem all the gifts he has given me to his glory. There's nothing wrong (and everything right) with enjoying the blessings God gives us. The trouble comes when we use them the wrong way. And convincing us to use God's blessing inappropriately is the devil's stock and trade.

In fact, the devil is a very easy master to please. He really doesn't care which sin we choose. He's cool with whichever side of the road we run off into. His job is simply to get us bogged down in the mud. But life is too short to spend it in a ditch on either side of the road.

What if we concerted our efforts to find glory and joy in whatever gifts God has blessed us with? For instance, if you have a high intellect, congratulations. Your intellect is a gift from God. The basic question is: How will you use it?

On the one hand, you may allow it to become a source of pride and arrogance. You find yourself unsettled when someone fails to introduce you properly without citing your academic achievements, and then referring to you as Dr. So and So. Or you may go off the road in the other direction. This would be when false modesty becomes your drug of choice. You fail to develop and use your intellect. You may wrongly believe yourself to possess a greater level of spirituality by demeaning the gift God has given you. In either case the devil is grinning.

Yet, on the other hand, you may select to foil the devil and make God smile by humbly acknowledging your abundant grey matter for what it is: a wonderful gift from God. Then with single mindedness, you determine to use it to his glory. You never brag, or make others of us who are less endowed, feel small or foolish. But you never hide or deny your talent either. You take rightful joy in being able to lead, advise, and assist others who need your wisdom.

The devil is the god of extremes and bi-polar spirituality. Our God is the Master of balance.

8

CHOOSE GOD CONFIDENCE OVER SELF CONFIDENCE

A llow me to postulate a premise that does not sit well with our politically correct, self actualized, and over indulgent culture. That premise is this: Possibly we have made a drastic mistake to tell two generations of American children that their goal should be to have a high level of self confidence. I've watched over recent decades as we have gradually stopped tapping little ones on the tush and saying, "That was a bad thing to do, Freddy!" Today, young parents agonize over whether it's even wise to send their little monster to the corner for a time-out, worried that it might damage his self esteem if they tell him that biting a buddy on the finger is not acceptable.

The Bible is replete with warnings about pride and arrogance—sometimes what we refer to as self-confidence. Parents are urged in Scripture to step up to the plate and do their job: "Discipline your son, for in that there is hope; *do not be a willing party to his death*" (Proverbs 19:18, emphasis mine, NIV). I like this particular passage because it speaks of both causal behavior and resulting outcomes. The writer reminds parents of their God-given mandate to discipline early while "there is hope." Why? So, as a parent, you won't bear responsibility for the inevitable ruin that comes to children who grow up without loving discipline. Life (and especially childhood) is too short to fail at this most important of callings.

Anytime people in leadership attempt to build self confidence by rewarding those who fail to perform at exceptional levels with the same trophies and grades that are received by the few who truly earn them, we are sending a damaging message to both groups. We are saying that your self esteem is more important than your actual deeds. This is a dangerous message!

Anyone who works in or visits our prisons sees the results of undisciplined living every time they go behind the walls. I'm convinced that many of today's worst criminals have no shortage of self confidence. What they lack is morality and respect for others! This is what happens when a culture tells everyone he is his own "god." If we each self confidently assert our own "godhood" who is to determine what is right and what is wrong? How can you claim that your belief system trumps mine? And, more importantly, how do we avoid chaos and anarchy?

So what's the answer? Could it have to do less with the "confidence" side of the equation, and more to do with the "self" side? I agree we should aggressively teach confidence, boldness, and optimism to every generation. But maybe, instead of telling ourselves that that confidence has its genesis in one's self, we should teach that our confidence is in (and from) God.

When we begin to reframe the issue in this way, good things happen. First, the pressure is off. At our core (and in our more truthful moments) we each realize how finite and imperfect we are. To believe that self confidence is the ultimate goal forces any thinking person to realize how precarious he is in an uncertain world. But when we recognize that there is someone greater in whom we can build our confidence, we have found the gold standard. Now we can relax and rest in the assured confidence that we can safely lean into any headwind.

I call this "God Confidence." It makes life easier. No longer am I forced to pump myself up with some trite psycho babble that I know begins and ends with my own limited abilities. God Confidence allows human dignity to return. I no longer have to compete or compare myself to others to find self worth. Suddenly I'm at eye level with all of God's people. I am no more, or less, worthy than they are. My value is founded and grounded in God—not myself. I don't have to look up to anyone. And I mustn't dare look down on anyone either.

9

BE STRONG

When you think about it, most every cause and culture has its own flag. For instance, most Americans take pride in putting their hands over their hearts and pledging allegiance to the flag of the United States. Most schools have a flag that is waved at ball games. Each of our fifty states has a flag. And on it goes.

In a way, a flag cements and validates a cause. It is the visual proof of something bigger than the individual parts that it represents. A flag recognizes that there is a peeking order—a hierarchy. When an individual salutes a flag, he is acknowledging allegiance to something greater than himself—and, in the process, subordinating himself to that greater cause.

Pondering the realities I see in the world around me, I've noticed that God set things up in a similar way in the animal world. He designed all the animals to accept a certain hierarchy. It's instinctive for little animals to run for cover when a predator gets too close. In many species a dominant male asserts his control over the flock, the herd, or the pride only when all the competitive male counterparts applying for the job have accepted the dominant male's authority.

But on a more profound level, we humans tend to resist this notion. We hesitate to acknowledge headship. Sure, we may salute certain flags and we recognize the concept of pre-eminence in the animal kingdom. But many of us do not want to surrender our wills. So we end up saluting the wrong flag—or no flag at all.

When God wired us up he essentially made us all free agents. He allowed us to be sovereign—gods of our own lives if we choose. He didn't force us into a fate we have no control over. Instead, he approached us with a loving hand essentially saying, "I am here to hold you, protect you, and discipline you in a way that will give you the greatest joy over the longest period of time. But the decision is yours."

Then the devil was allowed to make his pitch to humanity. It started in the garden when he convinced Eve that the "good life" was only a bite of fruit away. He convinced Esau that a bowl of soup (probably without even a stack of saltines) was worth his heritage and birthright. He convinced Peter that it was time to seize control of his own future—and deny his best friend with curses on the eve of Jesus' crucifixion.

Today, Satan is poised to seize the next moment of weakness in your life by trying to sell you the same bill of goods. When the company downsizing memo goes out, will you be willing to "dis" a fellow worker in order to keep your job? When friends at the clubhouse are complaining about their spouses, will you join in telling yourself that it's okay—after all "it's just a joke?" When you see the next attempt of a godless culture to further divorce itself from acknowledging our God in the public arena, will you go along to get along?

The apostle, Peter, had this same struggle. Early in his career with Jesus, he ran hot and cold. When the going was easy, he was squarely with Jesus. But, when questioned about his allegiance to Jesus on the crucifixion night, he lowered his "Jesus flag," buckled at the knees, waffled, and stole away into the night. Some days later Jesus told Peter that, in time, this would all change. In the last chapter of John, Jesus told Peter that there would come a time when he would willingly take his stand for the Master—even at the cost of his own life. According to tradition this all came true when, decades later, Peter and his wife, Concordia, both elected to accept death for Jesus rather than denial of Jesus.

Chuck Swindoll puts it well when he reminds us that life is short and being a living sacrifice is tough because living sacrifices keep trying to crawl off the alter. Maybe the key is for me to grow up like Peter grew up. Peter finally caught the vision. He realized that he could only salute one flag. Joy, balance, and purpose only happen when an individual realizes that, as Bob Dylan put it, "you got to serve someone."

HAVE A "THANK YOU, LORD" HEART

Here's an understatement: Life is busy. If you are like me, the 168 hour week you are presently experiencing is only about half of what you need.

Sometimes busyness and tight deadlines cause me to perform in a less than considerate way. I rush out in the morning without kissing Bonnie. I don't engage in meaningful conversation with friends. I forget to pet the dog. And, sadly, sometimes I forget to thank God.

There have been so many desperate moments in my life (as I would suspect there have been in yours) when I was left sucker-punched and gasping for air. The time we learned that our daughter, Megan, had a growth on her spine. The day that we learned that our largest client had filed bankruptcy and the future of our firm was in some question. The doctor's visit that began with the words, "This isn't going to be a very pleasant meeting."

Stop for a moment and force your mind back to a similar situation in your own life. Maybe you don't have to think very hard. Maybe your immediate response is, "Steve, I'm in the middle of one of those moments right now! And, frankly, it doesn't feel like a moment—it feels like an eternity."

If your behavior in such experiences is like mine, three things may be true.

First, in the middle of the storm you are completely and totally given over to God. You suddenly become very religious. You spend every moment you can spare breathing a prayer. The minute you get home you rush to your bedroom, shut the door, and fall before God pleading with him for the help you cannot supply from your own strength. Maybe you are even tempted to "bargain" with God: "Father, if you will only grant me this one request, I will never do this or that again." At first you worry about the way you form the words of your prayer. "Am I saying this correctly—did I include all the 'right' words to get through?" But soon, your prayer goes from clearly formed sentences to moans and whimpers that can only be understood by the Spirit of God. You feel totally wasted when you finally stand to leave the room. You wonder, "Did God hear me? What will he do?" Then, immediately you chastise yourself for having such a "faithless" thought—and hope it doesn't somehow negate the prayer you've just prayed.

Sometimes days pass seemingly with no answer—no resolution. Often the storm lasts for weeks or even months.

However, in time, the second stage comes—a new morning! The Psalmist says, "Satisfy us in the morning with your unfailing love, that we may sing for joy and be glad all our days" (90:14, NIV). The phone rings and it's the doctor's nurse (thankfully not the doctor himself) to tell you that the tests all came back negative. Or the broker calls to tell you that the horrible loss in your retirement account was their mistake, and by day's end all of your money will be refunded. Or your spouse finally comes home with tears in his eyes, forgives you, and you melt into one another's arms. You are so relieved you hardly know what to do.

This is when we enter stage three. As life returns to normal, so do we. The shopping still has to be done. Then there's the Tuesday night bowling league. And don't forget the kids' soccer games. Suddenly, without even realizing it, we have put God back in the closet of our mind. We know he's there, but we treat him like a "tool" that is at one moment urgently needed then, with the emergency passed, put away and forgotten.

Too often this is exactly the way I've treated God. When the pressure and the passion have passed, my prayers end. It's as though someone has snatched me from the waves in the middle of an ocean and hoisted me aboard the safety of his ship—and all I do is ask, "Which way is it to the shuffleboard court?"

Following is a passage from Luke that is at once one of the happiest and one of the saddest passages in the Bible. Note the part I have put in italics.

> As he entered a village, ten men, all lepers, met him . . . calling out, "Jesus, Master, have mercy on us!" . . . he said, "Go, show yourselves to the priests." They went, and while still on their way, became clean. One of them, when he realized that he was healed, turned around and came back, shouting his gratitude, glorifying God. He kneeled at Jesus' feet, so grateful. He couldn't thank him enough . . . Jesus said, "Were not ten healed? Where are the nine? Can none be found to come back and give glory to God?" (Luke 17: portions of 12-19, The Message)

My God is not some tool in the back of the closet of my life. He is not my cosmic bell-hop. God is God. He loves me and hopes that I will love him back.

As the years of my life have fallen away, I've become increasingly dedicated to what military people call debriefing. When a mission is completed it is SOP (that's Standard Operating Procedure for you non-military types) to re-think, re-live, re-evaluate, and re-examine. It is time to reassess and remember all that has happened. And it is time to give credit to whom credit is due. In some cases individuals receive medals and awards.

I believe that it is my privilege and my duty not to forget God when morning breaks and the sun begins to shine again. When God has brought me through a storm, it seems the least I should do is to honor him with intentionality. I need to return to that same spot on the floor that soaked my tears just yesterday as I pled with God to lend the help that only he could supply. I need to muster the same level of passion that I experienced during the crisis. But, this time, turn it into joyful, abundant, abandoned praise, worship, and thanks.

We have great biblical precedent for this too. When God had blessed the Israelites' prayer for protection from their enemies, King David didn't return to the daily grind without praising God lavishly.

> "David . . . danced before the LORD with all his might . . . with shouts
> and the sound of trumpets . . . (When David's wife) Michal . . . saw
> King David leaping and dancing before the LORD, she despised him
> in her heart . . . David said to Michal . . . 'I will celebrate before the
> LORD. I will become even more undignified than this, and I will be
> humiliated in my own eyes.' And Michal . . . had no children to the
> day of her death. (2 Samuel: portions of verses 14-23, *NIV*)

So the question is pretty easy. When God blesses me—do I want to end up like David (a man after God's own heart), or like Michal? The choice is mine.

11

LISTEN TO OTHERS
WHEN YOU DISAGREE

All of us have been in a staff meeting, at a church gathering, or in a conference where someone presented an idea or perspective with which we disagreed. Not just a little bit. Oh no. This person's idea was the stupidest thing you'd ever heard! If you identify with this frustration, then what I'm about to share may be helpful.

I grew up with what sociologists are now calling a "modern worldview." Simply put, this means that I (like most people from the eighteenth century forward) believe that truth is absolute. And if an individual simply stacks up enough facts, it will bring him to an inescapable, undeniable, and indisputable conclusion. While I do believe in absolute truth, I also am aware that many people (predominately those under forty-five or so) don't share my worldview. They are known as "post-modernists." These people tend to believe that truth is relative. Some of this thinking harkens back to the 1960s and 1970s when we were told that "you're okay and I'm okay" and "if it feels good, do it." Summed up in a phrase, their life view essentially says, "What works for you is fine—but that same 'truth' may not work for me, and that is fine, too."

While I am not an apologist for postmodernism, I do think there are some lessons for us modernists to learn from our younger friends—and them from us. As I said, I do affirm a belief in absolute truth. But sadly, we modernists have gone to unforgivable extremes. In an attempt to "get it right" we have often allowed our fact-stacking to become the rankest form of legalism. And it's that very arrogance that has emboldened the postmodernist to throw the proverbial baby out with the bathwater. They look at those of my sort and say, "He has no passion, no soul. Everything is a matter of facts and data for that guy. What happened to his 'heart' and his imagination? Why is he not wondrously intrigued and mystified by the unknowable? Why does he claim to know more about God's will than God has chosen to tell us? Where is the heart and soul—the mystery—in his faith?"

Those, my dear modernist friend, are fair questions. If we are ever going to have connection and rapport with others, we must first understand the viewpoint of others. And to understand another, we must really hear what she is trying to say. This doesn't mean that I have to agree. But it also doesn't mean that I must disagree disagreeably.

As a stepping off point, I would suggest that differing with another person does not require (or permit) me to diminish or deny his personhood. Most people speak words that they believe are true, beneficial, and affirming. They may be wrong—but it's not always the wisest play for me to be the first to tell them so.

What if we did things differently? What if, instead of me protecting my own turf, I simply listened and pondered what is said? What if I made a concerted effort to look for the good, the positive, and the accurate in what he says? What if I sincerely searched for common ground?

I noticed this dynamic being played out in my own marriage a number of years ago. Granted, Bonnie and I are the same age and share a similar heritage. We're pretty much on the same page in most situations. We agree on the big issues. But that is not to say we haven't had our share of, shall I say, disagreements.

For the first years of our marriage I was an arrogant husband. Simply put: My way was right and Bonnie's way was wrong. Of course, I was never bold (or honest) enough to state that in so many words—but looking back, I realize that that it is the truth. I was frequently dismissive and disrespectful of Bon's positions and thoughts. But as the years passed, I finally began to shut up and listen more. And you know what? I began to learn stuff. I began to witness a depth of wisdom that I had ignored and squandered to my own hurt for far too many years.

Often, as I was trying to break down the front door of the house by beating on it (frequently the male's frontal approach to any challenge), Bonnie was quietly walking around to the back of the house, finding an open door, and walking through the house to open the front door that I was still beating on.

If we can simply learn to lead with the heart as we listen, relationships will improve. We may find that there is less distance between us than we thought. And when there are real differences that need to be discussed, we will have a bridge of relationship and mutual respect on which to travel from our side to the other. Paul was a man who had seen his share of conflict, yet as he grew in Christ he realized, "For God is not the author of confusion, but of peace" (1 Corinthians 14:33, KJV). Life is too short not to build relationship.

BE FUN TO BE WITH—JESUS WAS

A s I've warned elsewhere in this book, there is usually a danger in extremes. So, as I share this concept, it will require some caution. I certainly don't intend to be flippant, irreverent, or sacrilegious. I am fully aware of the sober, solemn side of our Savior. Isaiah foretold Jesus' biography this way, "He was despised and rejected by men, *a man of sorrows, and familiar with suffering*. Like one from whom men hide their faces he was despised, and we esteemed him not" (Isaiah 53:2-4, NIV emphasis mine).

Jesus lived up to his Old Testament billing. He was jeered, belittled, and mocked throughout his ministry. He often slipped away to the mountains or the beach to share his grief with the Father. Finally, he was murdered like the worst criminal and forsaken by his friends.

But I return to the word "balance." To leave our depiction of Jesus at this stage would be to ignore an equally real aspect of his persona. Jesus was fun. He was laid back. Unlike other rabbis of the day, Jesus hung out with commoners. He no doubt laughed at their jokes and told some of his own. He horsed with the kids—and apparently was not a worry to their mothers. I suspect they intuitively trusted that smile of his. Likely, one of the most compelling things about Jesus was that he laughed easy and often. I don't know how he looked. I can't tell you how long his hair was or whether he wore a beard. But

I like to think that by his early thirties, Jesus already had laugh lines. Frankly, what I miss most among the paintings of Jesus by the great masters are more pictures of him laughing, smiling, and slapping friends on their backs.

When we miss this aspect of Jesus, we also miss part of the man and his message. In a culture like the present, this is dangerous. People everywhere are at once longing for Jesus, yet trying to push him out of their lives. I wonder how much of this is because of the way Christians have represented Jesus to the world. Christ gets much of his worst public relations from those of us who should be most intent on putting Jesus' best foot forward. I wonder how many searching souls we have run off—not because they rejected Jesus, but because they found his kids to be such stinkers!

Over the years I've visited and spoken in hundreds of churches. One thing I learned early on was that you can tell a lot about a church's theology with a quick glance over the brochures in their foyer. In about two minutes you can tell whether they are seeker friendly, or trying to be as divisive and exclusive as possible. Quickly you can learn whether love reigns or legalism rules. It will identify what their beliefs are and which hang-ups they hold most dear. I will never forget a church in southern Alabama. I had preached a sermon on grace which was met with scorn by some of the members—and by disbelief by some of the less indoctrinated. At one point I wandered into the church's lobby to look around. I'll never forget one of their brochures. There it was, right out there for any potential convert to read. The title was something to the effect, *Why It Is Wrong to Have Fun in Church*. The little document went on to decry people who don't take church seriously enough.

Maybe we would benefit lost sinners (and some of us saved ones, too) by rethinking how Jesus mingled with his society. Certainly he had tough words for tough situations. But his harshest comments were reserved for the religious legalists who seemed to take joy in excluding everyone possible from the Kingdom. But in his moments with struggling sinners, Jesus was quite different. As a matter of fact, he went out of his way to go where they were—physically and emotionally.

Do you remember Jesus' first miracle? It was in Cana. Jesus, his mother, and the disciples all were guests at a wedding feast. Well into the festivities an embarrassed waiter realized that he had under ordered on the wine. The vats were empty and the people were still thirsty. Jesus, being made aware of the problem by his mother, didn't lecture the crowd about too much partying. He simply helped the party keep going by miraculously producing an entire new vintage from plain water. And apparently Jesus knew how to make the good stuff:

> When the headwaiter tasted the water which had become wine, and did not know where it came from (but the servants who had drawn the water knew), the headwaiter called the bridegroom, and said to him, "Every man serves the good wine first, and when the people have drunk freely, then he serves the poorer wine; but you have kept the good wine until now." *This beginning of His signs Jesus did in Cana of Galilee, and manifested His glory, and His disciples believed in Him.* (John 2:9-11, emphasis mine, NASB)

Notice two small comments at the end of the passage. First, we note that this was the miracle through which Jesus decided to introduce this new ministry of Good News from God. Jesus "manifested his glory" by keeping the party going. And second, we see what resulted. Jesus' decision to be a friend to the people caused his disciples to believe in him. Jesus was bold, audacious, and unapologetic. He was the life of the party.

Maybe if modern day Christians were more committed to joyfully biting into life's apple we would leave a more appealing mark on our non-believing friends. Some of the most effective ministering I've done has been done over a bar counter. Am I promoting drunkenness or suggesting that we compromise on the truth? Of course not. What I am promoting is the old concept our moms taught us. It had something to do with catching more flies with honey than with vinegar.

13

FORGIVE QUICKLY AND BE JOYFUL

I have never met a happy person who was unwilling to forgive. And I've noticed that those who do forgive seem to be able to weather the worst of storms.

A number of years ago, Nashville was rocked by the disappearance of nine-year-old Marsha Trimble. A few days later, she was found raped and murdered near her home. I can still remember watching the story unfold on the daily news. But for me (and I suspect many others) the most amazing aspect of the story was the response from Marsha's parents. Of course, both were devastated, but they were also forgiving. In various interviews the public marveled at how these parents were able to talk with compassion, and even forgiveness, about their daughter's murderer. Frankly, I'm not sure I could have done that.

The Trimbles reflected the soul of Jesus. I say this because as I learn more about Jesus, I learn more about his easy way of forgiving. Do you remember when Christ predicted that Peter would deny even knowing him on the eve of his crucifixion? Indignantly, Peter assured Jesus that he was wrong. But by the end of the night, Peter was sweating, swearing, and insisting that he had never been a friend of Jesus. This brings us to one of the saddest verses in the entire Bible: "Just then, the Master turned and looked at Peter. Peter remembered what the Master had said to him: 'Before the rooster crows, you will deny me three times.' He went out and cried and cried and cried" (Luke 22: 61-62, The Message).

Can you imagine that "look" from Jesus? It must have cut through Peter's skin down to his very soul. Peter must have thought, "That's it. Jesus has cut me off. I'm through."

But just a few days later, after his resurrection, Jesus appeared to seven of his disciples (including Peter) as they were fishing. Within moments, Jesus had engaged Peter in conversation—one that the apostle would probably have preferred to avoid. On three occasions the Master asked Peter if he loved him. Each time, Peter squirmed and (using another Greek word) responded by essentially saying, "Yes, Master, I like you a lot."

If I had been Jesus, by this point, I would have written this loser off. Peter would have been toast! I would have done the math and said to myself, "Peter has offended me for the last time. He utterly denied me three times as they were leading me to the crucifixion. And today, even with time to rethink his cowardly betrayal of me, he still won't grow a spine and tell me that he loves me. We are finished. He's off my speed dial!"

But oh no! That was not the Jesus style. Instead, Jesus accepted (and forgave) Peter. He simply said, "Tend my sheep." (Loosely paraphrased, Jesus lowered his expectation of Peter and said, "Okay. Come on and work with me on your level.")

You see, when Jesus forgives, he forgives totally. No holding back. No strings attached. No "penalty box." Have you ever been sort of forgiven by someone else? They really didn't forgive—they just put you on probation. You were in the penalty box until they said otherwise. That's not how Jesus did things.

In that same Bible story in John 21, Jesus opened a door and gave Peter a glimpse into the manner in which he would die, "'I tell you the truth, when you were younger you dressed yourself and went where you wanted; but when you are old you will stretch out your hands, and someone else will dress you and lead you where you do not want to go.' Jesus said this to indicate the kind of death by which Peter would glorify God" (John 21:18, 19b, NIV).

Apparently Peter got the message. According to tradition, Peter and his wife, Concordia, lived out their lives in faithful, unashamed service to God. Then, many years later, Peter was given another chance to duck and run. But Jesus' forgiveness had made its mark in Peter's life. This time Peter didn't run. Instead, he faced his own executioners in Rome. Before they forced him to watch his wife be murdered, Peter held Concordia's hand and said, "Remember, dear, our Lord." Then, with Concordia dead, they turned to Peter who simply requested that, since he was unworthy to die like his Master, that they crucify him upside down.

We've all been wronged. But less remembered by many of us is that we have, also, all wronged others. Maybe this was the Trimble's secret. Maybe they realized how much they had been forgiven by their Master. And by extending forgiveness, they gained in two ways. First, by leaving vengeance to God, they reduced their own stress—and probably lengthened their lives. They realized that life is too short to live it with hatred. Second, their gracious behavior was so atypical that it forced people from all walks of life to wonder, "What do those parents have that I don't have? Are we missing the big picture?"

14

REMEMBER PAST BLESSINGS

Several months ago, I was totally bummed. It seemed that life was falling in on me. Nothing was the way it should be. Among other things, I had lost my voice. And this wasn't a three-day bout with laryngitis. The doctor had informed me that I had a hemorrhaged left vocal cord. For someone who makes his living as a public speaker that's serious! For most of four months I wasn't allowed to say a word, cough, or even clear my throat. Bottom line: I was doing a lot of whining.

At some point through this period I finally came clean with my best friend (and bride of thirty-three years), Bonnie. I complained about my predicament. I told her how ticked-off I was. I communicated that I wasn't even sure that God was hearing my prayers.

Bon has always been more spiritual than I am. Maybe that's why she tends to remain calm when I'm red-faced and those things on the side of my neck are bulging out. In times like these, Bonnie's first comment often starts with the phrase, "Well, the blessing in this is so and so." Bonnie has a way of seeing the good in the bad. She has the ability to look down the road far beyond where human eyes can go. She has spiritual eyes that depend more on Whom she knows than on what she is presently looking at. Bon has 20/20 vision of the soul. She is one of the few people I know who really gets the big picture.

That day, my best buddy gave me some advice. Fortunately, I was smart enough to take it. I've been glad ever since. Maybe, if you are more like me than Bonnie, this little strategy will serve you well, too.

First, let me share the back story. (You can read the full account in 1 Samuel 4-7.) Here's the *Readers Digest* version. It all goes back to a time about 1100 years before Jesus was born. Things with the Israelites weren't good. Most of their problems were self-inflicted because of their disobedience to God. They were in constant battle with five Philistine kingdoms. And with over 30,000 battlefield deaths, the people had given up hope. Even Eli, the old judge, had fallen over dead from the bad news. The Ark of the Covenant, their most cherished symbol of God's presence, had been stolen by enemy forces. For years things went from bad to worse. In the words of the widow of one of the priests, "The glory has departed from Israel." Finally, after decades of humiliation with the nation flat on its back, the Israelites finally began to look up—and repent. In his love, God gently wrapped them in his powerful hand. Their situation began to improve, and their enemies were again on the run. Finally, after a decisive battle, and with Israel the clear victor, Samuel, the prophet, decided to act: *"Then Samuel took a stone and set it up between Mizpah and Shen. He named it Ebenezer, saying, 'Thus far has the LORD helped us.'* So the Philistines were subdued and did not invade Israelite territory again. Throughout Samuel's lifetime, the hand of the LORD was against the Philistines" (1 Samuel 7:12-13, emphasis mine, NIV).

What was this curious "Ebenezer" stone that Samuel erected? It was a monument like the monuments we have today. When you stop to think about it, many of our most important monuments were set up to help future generations remember something, someone, or some event that is too important to forget. Literally, "Ebenezer" means "the stone of help." This was Samuel's way to help the Jews remember the power of God and his unswerving love for their nation. He knew that by remembering their past, it would build faith in future times of uncertainty and doubt. I suspect that for scores, if not hundreds, of years Hebrew fathers often stopped before the Ebenezer stone and said, "Son, let me tell you a story about the goodness of our God."

Now, back to present day. This was exactly Bonnie's advice to me. "Steve," she said, "you're acting as though God has never proven himself to you before. What about all the answered prayers? Have you ever made a list of God's answered prayers in your life—your own Ebenezer stone? Then, you could look at it anytime the doubts blacken the horizon of your life—and see the glory of God."

Talk about a guy who really married up! That was a great idea. So I got busy. Sadly, I could only recall a small fraction of the prayers God has answered in my life. Still, I was able to make quite a list. Today, I carry my "Ebenezer List" in my Bible. And when the worries smash into the coastline of my life, I pull out that list and reacquaint myself with what God has done—which confirms what he will do again.

15

EAT YOUR PROBLEMS FOR BREAKFAST

Although the name of this chapter is inspired by a book title from twenty years ago, I still love that little phrase. One of the most human of all the things we do is try to avoid pain. No one wants to be hurt. For most of us, problems are the quicksand of life. They bog us down and stop our forward motion. Allowed to go unchecked, problems will kill our productivity, energy, passion, and optimism.

A recent survey indicated that nearly sixty percent of employees under age thirty-five want to be managers. But among employees over fifty-four, less than a third said they would accept the title of manager. As a guy who is in his fifties, and who has managed a number of companies, I can tell you exactly why the seasoned pros responded the way they did: They don't want the grief! Management seems prestigious and exciting to young, inexperienced workers. But as the years pass, reality and cynicism often set in.

However life is too short to spend our days running from its inevitable difficulties. In this chapter I want to share some strategies that will help you view problems from a healthier and more productive perspective—and learn to "eat them for breakfast."

It was several decades ago when I began to realize that problems have the potential for good. I noticed that a friend of mine (who was in a pressure

52

cooker job) rarely used the word "problem." Instead, he chose the word "challenge." When he hit a really rough patch of life waves, he would often say, "Let's think about what God is trying to teach us through these challenges." I noticed that he seemed to weather tough times better than most of the other people I knew.

Life has taught me that problems (or challenges) can be the precursor to great blessings. When I was twenty-seven years old I noticed that my left arm ached when I walked fast. I didn't think much about this quirk until I mentioned it to my doctor one day. His worried look concerned me. To make a long story short, that was when I learned that I have heart disease. By my thirties I would be informed that the disease had become significantly worse and that I would be having quintuple bypass surgery. Needless to say, that was not part of my life plan. I expected to live forever. And this was a real problem! Or was it simply a challenge?

It's now been nearly two decades since my surgery. And I can tell you truthfully that the experience has been a blessing on a host of levels. First, unlike most of my contemporaries, I learned early in life just how precious every day is. I may have been in my thirties chronologically, but in doggy years I was in my sixties. So I determined to use my time more wisely. Suddenly the mundane became important. Time with my family was a gift to be savored. I wanted to experience all that life had to offer.

Second, this experience forced me to grow up. I became more sober about what is really important. I began to separate the temporal from the eternal. My relationship with God became more urgent and vital. My prayer life has grown and grown. I also made up my mind to do all I could to slow the progression of my disease. I still remember my surgeon. Technically, he was great. But his bedside manner came up a bit short. Soon after my surgery he nonchalantly told me that I'd probably be sick again in four or five years. When I asked why, he explained that it was because my disease was serious and most people don't change their lifestyles—they go back to their bad behaviors as soon as the scare wears off. That was the day I determined to do otherwise. Since my surgery I have become a healthier person. I haven't had a steak in all these years. I work out vigorously at the YMCA and have lost weight. And I take my meds religiously. Anything could happen, but thank God, today I feel great!

Third, God has allowed me to use my illness to minister more effectively to others. The truth be told, I probably wouldn't have as much empathy for other sick people if I had not experienced my own illness.

Here's what I've learned: Essentially there are three ways to deal with a problem. I call these the "3 R's." The first is to "run away." The second option is to "resist it." The third is to determine to "resolve the problem." It won't surprise anyone when I tell you that my preferred "R" is to resolve the problem. But that's where the rub comes. Exactly how do you fearlessly stare a problem down and resolve it?

This is where a fourth "R" comes into play. I call this the Roller Coaster Strategy. Years ago, I was afraid of roller coasters. But it wasn't cool to admit such a "girlie" thing, so I jumped on and did my best to look like I was having a ball. All the time my white knuckles were gripping the bar tightly, and I was pushing as far back in my chair as possible trying to brace for the inevitable. It wasn't until some years later that I learned a whole new way to ride roller coasters—a way that made the experience a real hoot. Instead of dreading every turn and drop, I changed my attitude. I got onboard with my mind made up to really enjoy the ride. When the coaster would finally reach its highest point, I would let go, put my hands in the air, lean forward, and dare it to give me its best shot. Wow! Suddenly with the fear gone, I loved the rush. It was fun. Today, I am somewhat of a roller coaster connoisseur.

The fact is, problems (again, I prefer the word challenges) offer the chance for change. If we embrace the challenges that hit us we have the opportunity to grow. They can make us smarter and more careful. They can help us avoid even more painful situations. They can help us help others dodge some of the pitfalls of life. Many of the most effective ministries that I'm aware of were started by broken people. Often people who have weathered tough challenges (pornography, alcohol and drug dependence, divorce, etc.) are the most able to minister to others.

A number of years ago in a live presentation, I heard Zig Ziglar say, "Life is about getting the 'no's' out of the way." All of us will have plenty of painful "no" situations during the course of a lifetime. We're all going to be faced with good and bad. The goal is to see the bad as challenges from which we can grow the good.

16

BE PREPARED
FOR THE FUTURE

Most people have hobbies. Some folks collect stamps, or bottles, or used chewing gum. Other folks like to kayak or spend weekends climbing mountains. Me? I like radio and old time rock n' roll. As a kid I hung out at the stations near my home. By my teens I was on-air "spinning the records" myself. I worked at various radio stations during college in the 1970s. Then, for a few decades I owned a record label and a radio production company. More recently, for a while in the 1990s we did *Coast to Coast Gold*, a nationally syndicated show where I got to play the old music and interview the folks who'd made it.

It goes without being said that I liked some of the music, I loathed some of it, and I loved a little bit of it. There are a few select songs from that magical era that will always be a heartbeat away from my lips. Something magical happened when those particular songs hit the record grooves—and music was born that will never die.

It was the hot summer of 1966 when one of the coolest records of all time hit #1. The song was from a new group called *The Happenings* (how much more 1960s could a band's name be?). You know how some songs take a while to grow on you? You have to hear them several times before you begin to like (or should I say, dig) them. It wasn't that way for me with this song. This one

was special. Maybe you remember it. It was called "See You in September."
It's the story of a young man who is about to leave school for the summer.
He is asking his girlfriend if she will stay true to him while they are apart.
He reminds her that he will be by himself every night. Then he asks her to
remember him and to write often. He encourages her to have fun, but begs her
not to flirt with other guys. Finally, he concludes with the haunting question,
"Will I see you in September, or lose you to a summer love?"

When I first heard this song, my adolescent mind pictured a star-crossed
couple as they said goodbye for the summer, and the boy as he asked his girlfriend to stay true and return to him in September. But one day something
far more profound dawned on me. This is exactly what Jesus is saying to us.

He's telling us of his loneliness and desire to be united with each of us.
And he's reminding us that while we're separated (the physical from the eternal) he wants us to stay in touch. He longs for us to "write," or pray, regularly.
He wants to hear all the details of our lives. He wants to know when we've
had a bad day—or a good one. He's concerned when we're sick, or worried,
or lonely. He wants to know when a relationship has fallen apart. Also, he
really wants us to have a good time during our "summer" here on earth. Jesus
is no killjoy. He loves for us to drink in the joys and taste the delicious beau-
ties he has left for us. But, at the same time, he wants us to remember that in
everything that is good, there is potential for evil. He doesn't want us to fall
in love with the here and now. He doesn't want us to develop a "summer love"
for the things of this world and become distracted from his call on our lives.

This is the message of Jesus to all of us:

And the God of all grace, who called you to his eternal glory in Christ,
after you have suffered a little while, will himself restore you and
make you strong, firm and steadfast. (1 Peter 5:10, NIV)

So watch your step, friends. Make sure there's no evil unbelief
lying around that will trip you up and throw you off course, diverting
you from the living God. For as long as it's still God's Today, keep

each other on your toes so sin doesn't slow down your reflexes. If we can only keep our grip on the sure thing we started out with, we're in this with Christ for the long haul. (Hebrews 3:14-14, The Message)

My personal goal: I want to be ready to meet my Jesus when the "summer" of this life ends—and the "September" of forever begins.

17

BE A PERFECT PERSON

How would you respond if I told you that I am perfect? Would you snicker or laugh out loud? Maybe you'd simply write me off as a fool and go on with your life. Well, I hope you won't do any of those things, because here goes: I, Steve Diggs, am perfect.

Now bear with me for a few moments and I'll return to that statement. But first let me be very clear in telling you that I have committed a smorgasbord of sins in my life. I have frequently been very disappointed in my own wife's husband.

To make some sense of this (believe me, this will prove a very important concept on your life journey) let me take you back to about 1971. I was in college. Frankly, for the most part, college bored me. (It really wasn't the college that I disliked—it was all those pesky classes that took me away from other things.) But there were a few classroom lessons from those days that I will never forget.

One of those lessons occurred when Dr. Carroll Ellis (head of the speech department and a minister) looked out at our religious studies class and proclaimed with his hand waiving in the air, "Sometimes people ask me if I practice what I preach. I always tell them, 'Noooooo, I don't practice what I preach because when I start practicing what I preach then I will begin preaching at a higher level!'" This was Dr. Ellis' way of admitting that, while he preached perfection, he had not achieved it. Then, with a touch of ironic humor, he suggested that if he ever attained the perfection he preached—he would be forced to preach an even higher level of perfection. Point: No one is ever going to achieve perfection through their own efforts.

Wow, something actually worth thinking about in college. I left class that day replaying Dr. Ellis' words over and over. This was new ground for me. Where I'd grown up, the general understanding was that preachers were perfect people. And very few ministers in those days made any attempt to dissuade others of that belief. But here was a minister not only admitting that he wasn't perfect—but telling a bunch of college kids that he didn't always even practice what he preached. Astounding! Imagine what I could have done with that one admission had the cell phone and YouTube been invented.

But somewhere down deep inside my soul, the point he was trying to make began to resonate. That single comment from the now deceased professor still pricks my soul.

If preachers weren't perfect maybe that meant that I didn't have to be perfect either, I reasoned. But Paul had already cut this theory off at the knees when he warned the Romans: "What shall we say then? Shall we continue in sin, that grace may abound? God forbid" (Romans 6:1-2b, KJV). And what was I supposed to do with Jesus' admonition: "Be perfect, therefore, as your heavenly Father is perfect" (Matthew 5:48, NIV)?

So Dr. Ellis must have been wrong. According to Jesus (who trumps Dr. Ellis any day) am I not supposed to be perfect? So I strived to be that way—perfect. But no matter how hard I tried, the pieces never fit. I always came up short.

Yet gradually, my meditation began to grow into fruitful realization. I started to pick up on what I believe Jesus meant. Since my Savior tells me to be perfect, then it must be possible to be perfect—right? Well, yes and no.

I was never a star student of the Greek language. (Just to get through, I bought off the smartest student in the class—convincing him to be my tutor in exchange for me doubling him on my motorcycle to the pizza parlor.) But I do know this much: The word Jesus uses for perfect comes from a Greek word that also has to do with the concept of going on to maturity or completion. So was this what Jesus meant when he said to be perfect? Maybe.

But I believe that what the Master really meant was even more profound. He meant exactly what he said, "Be perfect." But how? How can I ever be perfect? Gradually I grew to realize that in the DNA of Dr. Ellis' proclamation was a deep understanding of Jesus' directive for perfection.

Today, I boldly claim to be perfect. But again, before you write me off as a lunatic or a liar, let me explain why I am perfect—and how you can be perfect also.

Perfection only comes when I realize how totally and utterly unable I am to be perfect. That despair leads to the next question, "How can I fix my problem?" Which leads to the resulting answer, "I can't."

Stay with me here. This is the critical moment that saves a sinner. This is when he finally decides to stop nickeling and diming around with Jesus. He stops promising himself, "Yes, someday I'll accept Jesus and be baptized, but first there are some things I need to 'fix' in my own life." Here's the news: If you could "fix" yourself—you wouldn't need Jesus.

That's the moment when I realize that I have no goodness of my own. I have nothing, zero, zip to offer Christ. This is when I finally fall helplessly into the arms of Jesus. This is when Jesus accepts me. And God, in turn, seeing Jesus when he looks at me—accepts me too. And since Jesus is perfect (and since God only sees Jesus when he looks at the "new" Steve) in God's eyes I am perfect too. No brag—just fact.

18

BE QUICK
TO APOLOGIZE

We speak fondly and gratefully about what Tom Brokaw has called "The Greatest Generation." These were the young people of the early forties who gave up their own youthful dreams and fought a world war. Their efforts are the basic reason that we don't speak German or Japanese today. These were tough people who grew up believing in hard work and discipline. Sadly, my baby boom generation (and those who've come after) has never mastered some of the finer points of that elder generation's culture.

But I have noticed one tendency common among people from that great generation. As a group, many of them don't find it easy to apologize and admit fault—especially to someone who is younger.

I promised to be honest with you in this book, so I will honor that commitment as I share something that I have never written about before. One author, when asked if it was hard to write a book, said, "Not at all. All you have to do is open a vein." Well, here is where I must pull out a razor and become painfully personal.

My mother was one of the godliest women I have ever known. Before I was born, she quit her job as a teacher to become a 24/7 mom. Some of my earliest memories are of sitting on Mother's lap as she read us Bible stories. She always put my dad and us children first. She was always at home when

I came in from school—with a plate of cookies and an RC Cola. She served everyone she knew. When we were finally off to college, Mother made food for the lonely, visited the sick, and built a successful Christian pre-school. She was as close to perfect as a mother will ever be. But, with that said, she had a flaw. Mom could not make herself admit wrong and apologize. Sure, occasionally she would make a sweeping comment like, "Oh, I'm sure I've made mistakes." But I don't recall a single time when, of her own volition, Mother ever sat down beside me and simply said, "Steve, I mishandled that situation and I'm sorry. Will you forgive me?"

I wish she had. It would have improved our relationship tremendously. It would have lessened my adolescent frustration, anger, and rebellion. I knew she wasn't perfect. My dad knew she wasn't perfect. I imagine she knew she wasn't perfect. But, by not willingly admitting it, resentment grew. To the day of her death, Mother could never bring herself to deal with this problem.

On balance, I probably have not been as good a father as she was a mother. But one thing we determined to do early and as often as necessary was to apologize to our children. There have been scores of times over the years when Bon and I messed up with the kids. Often we didn't realize it until one of them pointed the fact out. And, too frequently, I allowed my pride to dominate. There have been times when I denied my mistake—or got mad at the child who was impertinent enough to make such an observation. But in most cases, it finally sunk in and I realized that I had dropped the ball. I needed to stop everything and go to that child and say the simple words, "I'm sorry. I really blew it and I hope you will forgive me."

Did this make us perfect parents? Not at all. But it did make us a little less imperfect.

We noticed almost immediate benefits from this approach. A gentle word really did turn away wrath. It had a soothing, calming effect on the children. It's hard to stay mad at a parent who is willing to apologize. A sincere "I'm sorry" is one of the most disarming phrases one can utter. Maybe this is part of what the Lord meant when he told fathers, ". . . do not exasperate your children; instead, bring them up in the training and instruction of the Lord" (Ephesians 6:4, NIV).

But more importantly, it helped to foster deep bonds and profound friendships with our now adult children. Over the years they have thanked us for being willing to apologize and admit our faults. But the greatest blessing has been to Bonnie and me. Today each of the four adult kids comes to Mom and me regularly to discuss their problems, dreams, and relationships. Sometimes their nakedly open honesty leaves us dismayed. They confess their sins to us and ask for prayer and guidance.

Apologizing quickly goes far beyond the parent/child relationship. As Christians, we need to be ready to admit guilt and apologize whenever the Spirit prompts us. When we make mistakes, it's wise to step up and make things right—before someone demands it. "If you enter your place of worship and, about to make an offering, you suddenly remember a grudge a friend has against you, abandon your offering, leave immediately, go to this friend and make things right. Then and only then, come back and work things out with God" (Matthew 5:23b-24, The Message).

Nope, I can't promise that this neat little formula will always make for a happy-clappy, problem-free, no-fuss-no-muss life. But if you model honesty, vulnerability, and a confessional heart, don't be surprised if you see the same reflected back to you one day. Isn't life too short not to give it a try?

19

START SMALL IF YOU HAVE TO, BUT START

As a habit, I don't put bumper stickers on my car. It's partially because they distract from the appearance of the car, but there's actually another reason why my car is a sticker-free zone. Frankly, I don't generally prefer to go around announcing all my political beliefs and preferences to a world that mostly doesn't care—and when it does, can become hostile.

But what about those bumper stickers that tell the world that I'm a Christian? You know the ones. Sometimes they're in the shape of a fish. Others make a proclamation of belief in Jesus as the Way to God. Why don't I put those particular stickers on my car? After all, if I'm really serious about Jesus, don't I want to be a walking, talking billboard? Isn't life too short to miss such opportunities?

This is where it's going to get a bit tougher, because this is going to force me to admit an embarrassing truth. I don't put those bumper stickers on my car because I'm afraid I'll do something that will destroy my witness. I'm afraid I'll do more harm than good. What if I cut another driver off in traffic, or lose my temper and glare at someone? Do I really want the last thing they see as I pull away to be a sign advertising my allegiance to Jesus? It's the same reason I don't wear many "Jesus shirts." I love and respect other Christians who attach the bumper stickers and wear the clothes—as long as they are really representing Jesus. But as I say elsewhere in this book, Jesus gets some of his worst PR from professing Christians who don't live their profession.

Recently I was working on a project with one of my dearest friends, Pat Boone. One thing about Pat—he's not ashamed to proclaim his faith. As a matter of fact, he wears neck chains and rings with godly symbols all the time. One day as we were wrapping up some work in his den, Pat pulled out a ring and said, "Steve, I have a gift for you." I wasn't quite sure how to handle a guy giving me jewelry. But in a moment I saw what it was: a beautifully designed ring with a very large cross in the middle—just like the one Pat was wearing.

Ah, this was perfect for me! Not as bold as a bumper sticker or as bombastic as a tee-shirt—but at least it was something. It was a start. So I thanked Pat profusely and accepted the gift. As I put the ring on my pinky, I decided that this would be my first witness to the world, so I turned the cross outward.

Since that day, I've worn my cross ring 24/7. As a matter of fact, recently a young woman at a cash register noticed it when I paid my bill. Over the months I'd seen her on a number of occasions. I had always been amiable and friendly. She said, "I really like your ring." I thanked her politely and walked on. Was she another Christian who had been encouraged by my ring? Was she a seeker who had run me through whatever litmus test she uses to assess whether Christians are real or fakes? I don't know. But at least in that one particular case, I was able to smile in my heart as I walked away knowing that I had acted like Jesus would want me to act. I had not embarrassed my Master.

Now for you Christians who are much more mature than I am—those of you with fifteen "Jesus stickers" on your car, a gold cross chain around your neck, and an "I love Jesus" tee-shirt with Scripture verses on both front and back panels—my baby step probably sounds pretty pathetic. But for me it was a start.

Maybe it would do us all well to realize two things:

1. Life is too short not to be a walking, talking, living, breathing banner for Jesus.
2. Life is also too short not to walk the walk if we talk the talk.

Frankly, this is sort of exciting for me. Who knows, it may help me graduate to a bumper sticker—or even a tee-shirt.

20

EMBRACE CHANGE

L ife is too short to waste it worrying about change.

Does change scare you? It scares most people. Much of my life has been spent trying to avoid change. I know psychologists have plenty of theories on the matter, but for me, I most dislike change because I don't know what will come next. And my fertile imagination has a way of dreaming up the worst possible outcome and multiplying it to the tenth power.

A little strategy that has helped me to cope with, and actually anticipate, change involves renaming it. Marketing people have long understood the importance of words. For instance, we no longer have used cars. Now they are pre-owned automobiles. And instead of TV reruns, my summertime shows are now called "encore presentations." It's the same with change. Maybe a different name would also bring a new vantage point. So instead of calling something a change, we could call it what it actually is: a life passage.

This morning as I begin writing this, I am preparing for a life passage—I think. At 11:30 I'm due to meet with Kevin for lunch. Our daughter Emilee and Kevin have been dating for some time now. Bonnie and I have expected what I believe is going to happen at lunch. Kevin came to my office the other day and asked for this lunch meeting. Immediately, I gulped emotionally and said, "Sure. When and where?" Frankly, I didn't care when and where—I was mostly preparing myself for the "what" of the meeting. You see, I think Kevin is going to ask me for permission to marry Emilee.

Now, there are several ways I can deal with this. I can become possessive and resist the entire notion. This would be a certain way to insure Emilee's eternal love for her dad. Yeah, right! Or I could wax emotional and relive the early years when we called Emilee "Porcupine." (It was because, back then, her now long, beautiful hair stuck straight out—like a porcupine.) Or maybe I could approach this with all the joy and optimism it deserves and realize that this is simply another life passage.

The reason I prefer this phrase instead of the word "change" is because it denotes the possibility of a new and beautiful vista—something I've never seen or experienced before. This is the optimism with which I believe God wants his children to approach life.

Why does the announcement of a new office manager scare you? Probably because you're worried she'll be worse than the last one. Why are you uncomfortable with the thought of having to move? Maybe because you assume that you'll lose old friends—and never replace them with new ones. Why would a parent be a bit apprehensive about a daughter getting married? Assuming the beau is as cool and godly as Kevin, only because things in the future won't be like they were in the past.

This is where "What if?" thinking begins to shine. What if that new office manager sees your talents in a light that her predecessor never did—and promotes you? What if your move leads to a new circle of friends whose depth and relational skills exceed anything you've ever before experienced? And won't those trips back for long weekends with your old friends be neat? And what if Kevin becomes wealthy and decides to buy Bonnie and me a home in Palm Beach? Well, that may be a little over the top, but you get my drift. There have been so many times after fighting and clawing to stave off a change—which is unavoidable anyway—that I was stunned at how much better things became.

In my experience, attitudes tend to become self-fulfilling prophesies. I still remember the old story of a man who was sitting in front of a general store. An out-of-towner pulled his car up, stopped, and said, "I'm thinking of moving here. What sort of people live in this town?"

Without stopping his whittling, the first man simply inquired, "Tell me about the people where you come from."

The traveler grumbled, "Oh, they were the worst! I never found a single person in that town who liked me."

"Those are exactly the kind of folks who live here," came the native's reply. "I'd recommend that you look somewhere else to homestead."

A short while later, another weary traveler pulled into town. He, too, saw the man in front of the store and asked the same question about the people of the town. Again, the local inquired about the traveler's previous relationships in his last hometown.

"Man, they were the best! Everyone in town was kind and ready to be a friend," he bragged, "I hated to leave."

Came the reply, "Friend, you're going to love it here too; let me introduce you around as soon as you're settled."

I wonder what would happen if "what if" thinking replaced the fear of change. Do you suppose that God would reward our faith and optimism with more peace, less stress, and greater eventual joy? Jesus said it himself, "As a man thinks, so is he."

PS: I'm back from lunch. It looks like we're going to get a new son out of the deal. I can't wait!

21

FIND YOUR GIFT

Let me paint you a picture of a child who has gone to a party and now feels left out because he notices that all the other children are playing with gifts from the host. Then, at the end of the day when his mother picks him up for the drive home, he breaks down and cries, "Mom, everyone else got a gift—except for me! Why didn't they give me a gift?"

Then imagine his disappointment when his mother seemed stunned as she looked in the rearview mirror and asked, "Didn't you go to the gift table and pick up the gift they had prepared for you?"

Life is too short not to find your gift. Yet that's how many of us live our entire lives. We never go to God's gift table to find what he has prepared for us. Let me share a few thoughts that may help you find and enjoy the gift God has waiting for you.

1. Be available to God's gentle promptings. Sometimes the key is simply to, "Be still, and know that I am God" (Psalms 46:10a, NIV). I believe that God has given everyone of us a natural bent. He has blessed each of us with abilities or inclinations that will lead our life paths to joyful conclusions if we will simply accept what God has waiting for us, and accept them on his terms.

2. Understand the nature of God's gifts. While I'm not convinced that it is an exhaustive list, Paul gives us a glimpse into the

heart of God as he names seven different "gifts of the Spirit" in Romans 12. (You can check them out for yourself, but briefly they include the gifts of prophesy, serving others, teaching, encouraging, giving, leading, and showing mercy.) God gives gifts so we can "re-gift" them. His idea is for us is to share and bless others with whatever our gift is—to pay it forward. Not to strain a metaphor, but I realize that this may seem like telling the same kid in the illustration above that he can go back to the party and retrieve his gift—but, then, he must share it with the other kids. Although it may sound counterintuitive, God's plan really does work best. He gives gifts (at least in part) so we can have the joy of blessing others. The happiest people I know are the ones who give the most.

3. Avoid cramming square pegs into round holes. Many of us spend our entire lives trying to be something that God never wired us up for. In high school and college days I was determined to get into show business. I reasoned (or rationalized) that I could do all kinds of great things for God if he would only allow me to become a famous star. By brute force and dogged determination, I eventually managed to sign a record deal with a major label and did several stage and television shows. But it never really fit me. Why? It was mainly because I had no real talent. I couldn't sing. (My voice has been known to kill small animals!) But for a long time, I resisted God's nudging. So I wasted valuable time trying to convince God to do it my way. Thankfully, he loved me too much to do so. I have long suspected that, had I succeeded in show business, I would have long ago left Jesus.

4. Avoid jealousy. Don't look at another Christian and say, "I wish I could sing or lead or communicate like he does." God's gift for you will be as unique as your finger prints—he knows what

will fit you the best. He knows exactly how much to give you;
and when to hold back—to protect you from yourself. This is
where trust comes into play.

5. Look for the "sweet spot." One way of knowing when you
   are ensconced in God's perfect plan for your life is that there
   will be a sense of peace and purpose. Paul called it "the peace
   that passes understanding." It's like that perfect golf swing
   (of which I've had very few). You know the instant your club
   makes contact that all is well as the ball flies freely and effort-
   lessly exactly where you intended.

When I start to see God's big picture for my life, things change for the
better—forever. There is a blessing when we "wait for the Lord" because we
"will gain new strength" and "mount up with wings like eagles . . . run and
not get tired . . . walk and not become weary."

22

BE GENEROUS
WITH MONEY

Without apology, I include in this book some thoughts about our money. After all, the Bible is full of financial advice. By one count there are over 2,200 passages in Scripture dealing with money and materialism. According to my wife's research, fourteen of Jesus' thirty-eight parables involve money. So it follows that big picture thinking means we need to get it right with our money.

The trouble with money is that we get a lot of misinformation from our culture about it. There's a lot of what I call "money noise" out there. Television has always filled countless hours of time with shows promoting the idea that money and happiness are synonymous. In the 1950s it was *The Millionaire*. By the 1980s we were watching *The Lifestyles of the Rich and Famous*. More recently, Regis wants to know *Who Wants to Be a Millionaire?*

Paul told his young protégé, Timothy, "For the love of money is a root of all kinds of evil. Some people, eager for money, have wandered from the faith and pierced themselves with many griefs" (1 Timothy 6:10, NIV). But that begs the question: What is the love of money? And that in turn leads to a host of other questions: Is it wrong to have money and wealth? Should Christians strive for "the things" of the world? Or should we disavow all earthly pleasure and focus solely on an eternity of joy with Jesus?

Again, this is where we can miss the point. Sometimes Christians get on television and encourage their followers to "name it and claim it," or, as I prefer to say, "blab it and grab it." This greed-based theology wouldn't fly in any country in the world other than America. Any Christian who dared postulate such heresy in a Third World country, where Christians are barely hanging on by their fingernails, would be laughed to scorn. On the other hand, I don't believe that God expects us to live in orange crates. So where is truth on this issue?

I've long been grateful that Paul laid a lot of these perennial questions to rest in 1 Timothy. Here the apostle lays out an entire theology of wealth management for God's people:

> Command those who are rich in this present world not to be arro-
> gant nor to put their hope in wealth, which is so uncertain, but to
> put their hope in God, *who richly provides us with everything for our*
> *enjoyment.* Command them to do good, to be rich in good deeds,
> and to be generous and willing to share. In this way they will lay
> up treasure for themselves as a firm foundation for the coming age,
> so that they may take hold of the life that is truly life. (1 Timothy
> 6:17-19)

Let's take a moment and really look at what Paul tells Christians here. First, he acknowledges that there are Christians who are "rich in this present world." (I'm glad he included the "in this present world" part, so high-minded Christians couldn't claim that Paul was simply referring to spiritual wealth.)

Second, Paul proceeds to give a three-step "to do list" for these wealthy Christians:

1. He says that wealth should not be an excuse for arrogance. In
   God's economy, whether we live in an alley or on an avenue,
   there is neither rich nor poor—just broken people desperately
   in need of a savior.

2. Next, he warns against the tendency of most rich people to put their hope in money. Why? Because there is no security in money; as anyone who had a 401(k) plan in 2009 can attest, wealth is uncertain. It can slip though our fingers like dry sand on a windy beach.

3. Then Paul tells Christians to adopt a lifelong strategy of doing good. He puts an even sharper point on it by telling them "to be generous and willing to share." What does this mean? Simply what it says. We should search for opportunities to share our wealth. This goes against human nature. Studies indicate that, as people get richer and richer, they tend to give less and less. Instead, wealthy Christians ought to be the best tippers, the first to grab the check when they're with less affluent friends, and the most compassionate with those who are in true need.

But lest we still feel guilty for having wealth, note the little phrase in the text above that I put in italics: "*who richly provides us with everything for our enjoyment.*" The fact is, God wants us to enjoy the blessings he gives us. Whether it's financial wealth, a good mind, or a strong body, part of the reason we have the blessing is to enjoy it ourselves! That's pretty cool isn't it? God is no killjoy. He is abundant. He gives freely and smiles broadly when his kids enjoy his stuff. He just wants us to play nice in the sandbox—and share. Sound familiar?

23

PURSUE A RELATIONSHIP WITH GOD

I was wondering, do you suppose that God might not be as interested in religion as we are? After all, religion for religion's sake has never done the deal. "Am I saying that Christianity is not a religion?"

Of course not. Christianity *is* a religion. But I repeat, religion for religion's sake has never done the deal, closed the sale, or nailed down the lid on life's problems. Religion has brought us most of our wars—including the two that we're presently fighting overseas.

So I wonder, just what is God *most* interested in? If God could only have one thing with me—what would it be? To get from where we are to where we need to go, we must understand some things about God himself. These must be ironclad characteristics that never change or deviate—no exceptions and no excuses. These would be absolutes about God and his nature.

Let's think. What would some of these characteristics be? Let me put forward a few. God is God. He's in charge. He has the right to set things up any way he sees fit. He could have announced that "I am the King of the universe," or "I'm the Boss of the cosmos." But God didn't do that. He came to us where we were and spoke to us in a language we could understand. There's a beautiful scripture that says, "But when the fullness of the time came, God sent forth His Son, born of a woman, born under the Law, so that He might redeem those who were under the Law, that we might receive the adoption as sons" (Galatians 4:4-5, NASB).

I have always loved this passage. It is as though God realized that in humanity's infancy he had to deal with humankind like young children. It wasn't that he didn't love us. It was just the opposite. He loved us enough to be very firm and direct. Thus the Old Testament stories of God's swift and immediate punishments. He had to give his people a swat on the tush to get their attention and lead them away from disobedient behaviors. But with the passage of a millennium, at long last when we were ready to perform on a higher, more mature level (in the "fullness of the time"), God was finally able to do what he had longed to do for so long: lean back and let up on the reigns a bit. Just like human parents long to do, God was able to appeal to our better side—through gentle love. His word became flesh and entered into this world as our friend, big brother, and savior.

With his Son's arrival came a deeper appreciation that God wanted us to think of him as "Father." His message: "I am you're Father and you are my children." Sadly, many of us have heard this so often that it has lost its impact. But this was revolutionary stuff! This unprecedented depiction of deity was the ridicule of the Greek pagans and the stumbling block for the Jews. How could deity be our Father? How does that work?

And while I'm on the topic, let me go a step further. There are at least two places in the New Testament (arguably three) where we are told that when our relationship to our Father matures, it will become a relationship of "Abba, Father."

> For you did not receive a spirit that makes you a slave again to fear, but you received the Spirit of sonship. And by him we cry, "Abba, Father." (Romans 8:15, NIV)
>
> Because you are sons, God has sent forth the Spirit of His Son into our hearts, crying, "Abba! Father!" (Galatians 4:6, NASB)

And when I say "Abba," I'm not talking about the rock n' roll band. I'm told that the closest equivalent we have in English for this Aramaic word is "daddy." Now if in your family's economy, the word "daddy" is a flippant or disrespectful way to address your father, that is decidedly *not* what I'm discussing here.

I am the daddy in our family. If my kids willfully disobeyed me there were consequences! But becoming a daddy back in the 1980s helped me theologically. Suddenly, some of those Old Testament passages where the Bible says that the eyes of God are upon us stopped scaring me. For many years, my picture of God had been that of an aloof Being who was constantly keeping score, just waiting for me to make a mistake so he could drop-kick me out of heaven. But when we started our own kid farm in the early 1980s, my thinking began to change. I noticed that my eyes were on my kids. As a matter of fact, I was on my hands and knees crawling all around the floor with them. But I can guarantee you one thing; I wasn't watching them hoping they would make a mistake so I could throw them out of my home!

I suppose there were two reasons for my intense interest. For one, I didn't want them sticking their fingers in the sockets or otherwise hurting themselves. But the main reason I was watching my kids so closely was because I thought they were cool! I wanted to spend relational time with my babies. Today the kids are grown and gone, and I'm combing my hair with a towel. But I'm still the daddy and my eyes are still on my kids.

I have a feeling that maybe my God is the same way. He wants a little less religion, and a little more relation.

24

CREATE TEACHABLE
AND REACHABLE
MOMENTS

As I write this, it's about 7:30 am. I'm up, dressed, and ready for one of my favorite things—a bike ride. Now when I say "bike" I'm not talking about some wimpy, peddle-pushing, complete with a basket-on-the-handle-bars model. Oh no. I'm talking about my black, fuel-injected, 1360 cc, Harley Davidson Road King. You may have heard about the Terminator. They call me the Sermonator! This is that moment when I wish I could make one of those manly grunts like Tim Taylor used to do on *Tool Time*.

Yeah, yeah. I've heard all the jokes about bikers: What's the difference between a Hoover and a Harley? The location of the dirt bag. Or how about this one: A motorcycle is a vehicle with two wheels and a nut on top. I'm not trying to convert you into a biker. This is simply an illustration to help me make a much bigger, more profound point.

In fact, I do like my motorcycle, but what makes it special is what it has done for my relationship with the kids. All of our children have enjoyed riding with me on the bike. But the one who has really made these freewheeling miles most special is our youngest daughter, Mary Grace. In about forty-eight hours Mary leaves to go back to college. This will be the beginning of her junior year at a university that is ten hours away from Mom and Dad! I'm bummed. But Mary won't know it this morning, because in just a little while we're due to mount the old iron horse and go cruising. Mary has never lived a day of her life that wasn't overflowing with activity. She has more fun, friends, and things to do than any kid I know. She'll probably squeal in my ears as we ride—and serenade me with Beach Boy songs.

But there is another reason why Mary and I are going for this ride that she probably doesn't even realize. I'm hoping it will offer a teachable (and reachable) moment. Now, before I go further, let me explain why I put an emphasis on the word "reachable." There have been far too many times during my decades of fatherhood when I've been gung-ho about teaching an important principle, but I was buck stupid on how I went about it. I have a knack for picking the worst times to try to communicate important stuff to the kids. Mary (bless her heart) has never been shy about pointing out this deficiency in my skill set. So hopefully, today I will find that sweet spot—a reachable moment that, in turn, can become a teachable moment. Maybe when we stop for a snack, or to find shelter to let a rain shower pass, I'll be able to ask her about her walk with Jesus. Or maybe we'll discuss some of her spiritual questions. Possibly, God's Spirit will prompt me to share a nugget that will help her through a tough time that may arise in the next semester.

Ever since we had children, Bonnie and I have looked for teachable moments. We did the formal stuff of course. When the children were smaller we had regular family devotionals and Bible studies. And since Bonnie home-schooled all four, she was able to weave biblical teaching into many of their classes.

For me, it's been a bit of a challenge to find the perfect approach for each of these four strikingly different personalities. It's taken some real imagination. Joshua was always ready to talk about any spiritual topic. By the time he was about seven we would get up early some mornings and read the Bible, discuss what we were thinking, and have a cup of juice or coffee. For Emilee, some of our best conversations happened when some other life event had caused her to come home elated or defeated. Megan still teases me about how I would simply "pop up" at her college dorm or wherever she was on campus for a surprise visit, a cup of coffee, and some conversation.

We established this pattern of providing teachable moments very early in the kids' lives. One of the things that the kids loved the most was our "midnight fun-runs." This practice raised the eyebrows on some of the more traditional parents in our circle of friends. But so what. I wasn't doing it for them. I was doing it to build relationships with Megan, Joshua, Emilee, and Mary Grace. Midnight fun runs were a bit like what we used to call late-night refrigerator raids—on steroids. Here's how they worked: Occasionally, on a non-school night, I would wake up one of the children so we could "sneak" out of the house for a snack. (I found that using the word *sneak* added an extra dimension of excitement and intrigue.) Once in the car, we'd head for that child's favorite all-night eatery—ice cream, donuts, burgers and fries—it didn't matter. The point was, this was our special, "secret" nighttime fling. And the best part of these nocturnal trips was that they gave me a chance to teach important principles in a positive atmosphere.

Too often we wait until the flood of life's problems has crashed through the dam and is overwhelming our homes and families. By finding teachable moments all along the way, you can avoid many of the harsh, negative, combative, and destructive events of life. By pre-acting you will have to do far less reacting. If daddies would find moments to encourage their sons and daughters to be pure until marriage, there would be far fewer of those middle-of-the-night, gut wrenching, tearful conversations trying to decide how to deal with an unexpected baby. There wouldn't be as many frantic trips to the emergency room because of stupid behavior. In a phrase, we would spend far less of our time trying to put the toothpaste back into the tube of life.

From his earliest teachings to humanity, God has urged parents to parent: "These commandments that I give you today are to be upon your hearts. Impress them on your children. Talk about them when you sit at home and when you walk along the road, when you lie down and when you get up. Tie them as symbols on your hands and bind them on your foreheads" (Deuteronomy 6:6-8, NIV).

Well, Mary and I are back. We covered more than forty miles in the beautiful area south of Nashville. We stopped for pop and coffee. And we talked about lots of stuff. And no, I won't tell you what it was. That would be a betrayal of Mary Grace. But suffice it to say, I feel as if we covered some critical topics—and grew closer to one another and God in the process. And yes, she sang to me. Plenty of Beach Boy music—with a nice sprinkling of everything else from Bill Haley, to Elvis, to Motown. All in all, it was a good ride. Actually, I'd call it one of the best rides of my life.

25

LEARN TO LEAVE SOME MONEY ON THE TABLE

It was more than twenty years ago, when in the midst of a business negotiation, the fellow I was haggling with said, "I don't want to leave any money on the table." I'd never heard that phrase before, but I immediately knew what he meant. Loosely translated, he was telling me that he wanted to squeeze every possible penny out of the deal.

Frankly, I liked that phrase and gradually began to apply it in my own business dealings. I always tried to be fair and honest, but I did drive tough deals and I did try to maximize our profits. Now, don't get ready for me to apologize for that—because I still see nothing wrong with conducting business this way. At least, up to a point. Obviously, if you are negotiating with a younger, less attuned businessperson, you don't want to take advantage of their lack of knowledge. But driving fair, tough business negotiations is proper and good in many cases.

However, as the years have passed, I realized that I had gotten too good at this skill. While not being dishonest, sometimes I asked for more than was reasonable. I'm writing this to suggest that life is too short to approach every negotiation (whether it is in the business or professional realm or in the context of our personal relations with others) as a competitive battle to grab every possible inch of turf.

Isn't this exactly what we find so repugnant about the Wall Street types and commercial bankers who suck every dime they can from their corporations—and then bale out in gold-gilded parachutes adding another hundred million to their portfolios? I wonder if this is exactly how Bernie Madoff got into trouble. Maybe he began with good intentions, but greed and lust slowly morphed into a constant hunger for more and more. This, in turn, led him to never leave any money on the table.

In Luke we find Jesus making a curious comment: "Watch out! Be on your guard against *all kinds* of greed" (12:15, emphasis mine, NIV). I used to wonder why Jesus used the little phrase "all kinds of greed." This passage used to confuse me. I wondered, isn't greed greed? Doesn't it play out in the ugliest, rankest, most outrageous forms of human behavior? Yes, in some cases it does. Again, I would point you to the Wall Street shenanigans. But in many cases, it is far more subtle. I am beginning to believe that sometimes greed can simply be asking for more. It can be the attitude that says, "What's yours is mine; and what's mine is all mine." It has to do with the attitude that more is always better.

Since that day over twenty years ago, I have probably become a bit less interested in squeezing the other person until he squeals. Simply put, I don't want to be a pig at the trough. Frankly, one of the reasons I agreed to write this book is because I respect the publisher, Leafwood. To remain in business, Leafwood must turn a profit. So it is most appropriate for them to construct author contracts with an eye toward making income for themselves. But I was pleasantly surprised when they sent me their contract. Two things struck my notice. First, it was less than ten pages long—a fraction of the length that many of their competitors use. And second, it was fair. Authors everywhere tell horror stories of unfair and ambiguous publishing contracts that later made them feel foolish and cheated. Leafwood's was fair (sure, we negotiated a few points—I'm not stupid) and it was direct. They could have grabbed for more profit and so could I. But we didn't. We were both committed to getting this important message out to as many people as possible—and also committed to treating the other guy fairly.

Sometimes greed is most effectively combated with an "anti-greed" policy. God had no problem with wealthy landowners making a profit and living well—but he wanted them to "leave money on the table." In the earliest training, God taught his people, "When you harvest your land, don't harvest right up to the edges of your field or gather the gleanings from the harvest. Don't strip your vineyard bare or go back and pick up the fallen grapes. Leave them for the poor and the foreigner. I am God, your God" (Leviticus 19:9-10, The Message).

Hundreds of years later, faithful followers were still applying this teaching—and in some cases, going the extra mile. Ruth, a widow, was one of the benefactors of this mandate. To keep body and soul together, this young woman was gleaning grain from Boaz' field. When Boaz learned of her desperate situation, he left more "money on the table" than God had commanded. He directed his servants to befriend her and share their water. He went even further by telling his workers, "Let her glean where there's still plenty of grain on the ground—make it easy for her. Better yet, pull some of the good stuff out and leave it for her to glean. Give her special treatment" (Ruth 2:15-16, The Message).

So what was the outcome of this random act of kindness? Boaz pleased God. He got a trophy wife. And he fathered a son who became the grandfather of King David.

In the big picture of life, sometimes demanding less gets us more in the long run.

26

BE FLEXIBLE

As I've mentioned, I fly a lot. I almost always fly American Airlines because I'm a real fan of the company. (In another chapter I'll share more about why I have this affinity for American.) A few minutes ago I was at the Nashville airport awaiting the plane that I'm presently on flying at 20,000 feet. Before I boarded, Terrell, a friend of mine with American Airlines, stepped up to where I was waiting for the flight and showed me a chart. It explained a worthy fundraiser that American is sponsoring. I noticed that several well-known Nashvillians had donated various items (autographed guitars and so forth) to be raffled off to raise money for this charitable cause. Terrell said, "Mr. Diggs, we were hoping that you would give us an autographed copy of one of your books for our fundraiser."

Granted, it was flattering. Any author who tells you he doesn't appreciate being asked to sign a book is either lying—or much more successful than me. But there was a time when Terrell's request would have caused me a problem. Let me explain.

I don't believe in gambling. That means I don't do raffles. I'm also not a fan of state lotteries. Why? Lotteries are gambling. "What's wrong with gambling?" you ask. Gambling, as I see it, is a predatory behavior. Someone has to lose for someone else to win. And just in case I'm not being blunt enough, allow me to rephrase: I believe that state lotteries are a tax on the stupid and the broke. Christians don't need to be stupid or broke—nor should we take advantage of those who are. The reality is your chances of winning a major payout in a lottery are probably less than one in 8,000,000. There's almost a better chance that a flea will fly into your left ear and come out your right eyeball singing "Dixie" than there is that you'll win a major lottery. And yes, in our family we practice what we preach on this. To date, we've passed up on thousands of dollars of free college tuition money because it came from the Tennessee lottery. Going a step further (stay with me here because I'm getting to my point), I am no fan of casino gambling or horse betting either. Is it wrong to buy a lottery ticket? Frankly, I don't know. Maybe it's simply a matter of conscience, but for me, it would be.

But this isn't a diatribe on gambling. As we catch our collective breaths, allow me to refocus my point. What I really want to do here is challenge the way I (and maybe you) sometimes allow our religion to do more harm than good. I don't claim to have all the answers on what I'm about to present here. I may be wrong. This is probably a chapter that would be best viewed as simply a "thought sparkler"—something for you to chew further on and ponder.

Here's my point: Sometimes I work so hard to be heavenly minded (crossing all the spiritual "t's" and dotting all the spiritual "i's") that I become no earthly good. Since I don't approve of gambling, does it follow that I should have declined Terrell's request? Would "making a stand on principle" have drawn Terrell (who knows that I'm a Christian) closer to Jesus? Or would it have made Jesus harder for him to see?

Assuming that a number of my readers have already stopped reading (because of this heretical viewpoint), I'm going to wade in a bit deeper. Let's extrapolate this point further into what may be uncomfortable territory for some of us who have tried to live neat, clean, lives of "check-list Christianity." What happens when a friend needs to talk—in a bar? Is my precious reputation worth more than his needs? Do I remain pharisaically "pure" and refuse to go—telling myself that to do otherwise would compromise my witness? Or do I follow the Jesus model of going where the needy are? Remember, Jesus counted some of society's greatest sinners (prostitutes, tax collectors, and the spiritually unwashed) among his closest friends.

Here's what I'm realizing as I get older: Christian living is not always neat and clean. Sometimes it's messy and confusing. Sometimes we are left to wonder, "Did I make the right decision?" No, I'm not promoting a Joseph Fletcher-style of situational ethics here. If you've ever read any of my books or heard me speak, you know that I believe in absolute truth. What I'm *not* sure of is where to draw all the lines.

What used to be easy—simply towing the company line and condemning everyone who saw things differently than I did—doesn't always work for me anymore. For instance, I am not fond of gambling—but I also hesitate to do something that would needlessly end the dialogue that Terrell and I have begun to develop. After all, where does the Bible directly condemn gambling? I don't know of a single verse. Granted, when we link gambling to other things (greed, taking advantage of others, etc.) we can build a case of sorts against it—much like I did above. But here's another absolute: Jesus called me to make disciples everywhere I go (check out Matthew 28). How can I do that without being their friend? How can I do that if all he hears from me is a personal "position statement" that is so ethereal that it leaves him shaking his head saying, "What's wrong with Steve? Is he too cheap to give us a book to help some needy people?" My point is its fine and good to discuss nuanced points with mature, fellow believers. But there is also a place to meet the immature where they are. Today my greater fear is somehow shutting a door of opportunity to build a relationship that could be the only bridge that that other person will ever have to Jesus—based more on my personal biases and hang-ups, than on what Jesus would do.

By the way, I told Terrell that I would be happy to sign a book for the charity.

27

FORGIVE YOURSELF
AND MOVE ON

So you have a hard time forgiving (and forgetting) your past? Me too. As a matter of fact, I probably have the tee-shirt, the coffee mug, and the tattoo to prove it. Grieving about past mistakes is a problem I've struggled with for most of my life. So let's spend a few moments together and share some thoughts on this all-too-common problem.

First, I am assuming that you are a Christian. If not, then the guilt you feel is real. I didn't say that it's unforgivable—just real. (You might want to look at the chapter on "Be a Perfect Person" for some thoughts on this.) Second, like so much else in this little book, if you miss my heart, you are also likely to miss my point. It is not my purpose to turn liberty into license. Taken to the extreme, what I'm about to share can do more harm than good. However, I grew up in a world where many of the religious types so intent on keeping us away from wrong scared us to death of God. I believe from my core out that there is a very real need for deep, contrite, humble repentance in all of our lives. Why? Because we're all sinners. We break our promises. We let down the people who trust us. We allow our greed to drive our financial decisions. We brag and are prideful about things that are actually gifts from God. We break the confidences of our friends. We behave badly.

But there also comes a time when forgiveness and forgetfulness need to be extended *to* oneself *by* oneself. Some of us are better at apologizing than we are at forgiving ourselves.

As I get into this, let me make a sexist observation on this point. In general, I believe that this is a greater problem for women than it is for men. Being neither an anthropologist, sociologist, nor psychologist, I have no way to document this theory scientifically, but still I believe it to be true. As a matter of fact, I have conducted my own "research." Much to my wife's chagrin, I've performed a little test that illustrates how many women seem poised to apologize for practically anything—whether or not it's their fault. More than once I've told Bonnie, "A woman will apologize to furniture." What do I mean by that? Simply that for many women, if they bump into a chair, they are likely to say, "Oh, excuse me"—before they realize that it's not even a person! Like I said, I've tested this little theory in the field. More than once in a public place, like a supermarket, I have deliberately nudged my cart against a woman's cart in the store. Obviously, to any unbiased third party observer, *I* am the one at fault. But, almost without exception, the woman will look at me with an embarrassed face and say, "I'm sorry."

Brothers, and especially sisters, it's high time that we begin to extend some of the grace that we extend to others to ourselves! It is time to knock it off, get over it, and go on with life.

A number of years ago, an especially troubling and trying experience came my way in the business arena. I had sold a business to a dear friend of mine. Without going into the details, the business situation did not turn out how anyone wanted it to and because it hurt so many people, this was quite traumatic for me. I felt that I had been honorable in the whole matter, but there were people who didn't know the facts, and blamed me. Thankfully, those who had worked on the deal were Christians, and to a person, they all assured and re-assured me that I had done nothing wrong. But still, I couldn't lay it down. For months I grieved. I lost sleep for hundreds of nights. But one of the things that helped the most was when I asked for a meeting with the leaders at my church. In that meeting, Bonnie and I were totally open and frank. We told them of all my worries, self-doubts, and regrets. I admitted to having made mistakes. Frankly, I wasn't sure what they would say or do. But I will never forget what happened. After Bonnie and I poured our hearts out (and cried a bucket-full of tears) one of these wise, godly men stood up and walked slowly over to a white board on the wall. He picked up a felt marker and wrote three words: "Let it go." Then he walked back to his chair and sat down.

I won't lie and tell you that this pivotal moment stopped all of my worry. It didn't. But it did help me catch my spiritual breath and begin healing. Let me share three thoughts that have helped in my struggle to drive a stake in the heart of this monster.

1. It's important to discern the difference between the loving, healthy conviction that God brings to us through his Spirit and unhealthy worry. Remember that "God is not the author of confusion, but of peace." Anytime a worry lingers but doesn't resolve into a healthy, productive conclusion, it's a safe bet that God is not involved. It is very easy for us to stay preoccupied with negative stuff. Such a focus keeps us from being productive for God.

2. I appreciate the words of a man who himself had committed plenty of sins and hurt lots of people. Paul had jailed and murdered a multitude of Christians before he accepted Jesus himself. What a burden to carry! Can you imagine how many times he must have looked out at an audience and caught the eye of a woman whom he had widowed? How many young people did he preach Jesus to whom he had orphaned? And don't you suppose that Paul wondered over and over, "Paul, you hypocrite! What right do you have to preach when you are the worst of the bunch?" Paul had to deal with this. I suspect he frequently drenched his pillow with tears and filled his waking hours

with self loathing. But instead of melting into a pity puddle, he saw the big picture. These words from the good apostle have brought a lot of us through some deep waters. "Not that I have already obtained it or have already become perfect, but I press on so that I may lay hold of that for which also I was laid hold of by Christ Jesus. Brethren, I do not regard myself as having laid hold of it yet; but one thing I do: forgetting what lies behind and reaching forward to what lies ahead, I press on toward the goal for the prize of the upward call of God in Christ Jesus" (Philippians 3:12-14, NASV).

3. Lastly, I am learning to judge trees by their fruit. For instance, what if Paul was convinced that he was unworthy to minister? Who would have evangelized the first-century Greek world? Who would have written a dozen of the New Testament books? Who would I look to for real world advice on how to overcome worry when it tends to decimate me? Thank you Paul for showing me how to say boldly, "Jesus' grace is sufficient for even me."

28

STOP PETTING PIRANHAS

As I point out several times in the pages of this book, many of our problems, frustrations, failures, and disappointments are self-induced. In our more reflective moments most of us are aware of this fact. Each of us can think of bad decisions that have led to failed results both in our own lives and in the lives of others. Some of these dumb behavior patterns are so obvious we wonder why anyone would trip the trap. Why does a seventeen year old boy fly through a busy intersection at 70 mph? Why do we overeat and under exercise? Why do people destroy their sex lives in marriage with internet porn? Even if you are personally guilty of similar bad choices, you will still admit that there is really no ambiguity here—these are clearly destructive behavior patterns. Right?

I want to delve into another destructive behavior that sneaks up on some of the best and brightest among us. I call it petting piranhas. Simply put, it's trying to have a relationship with someone who doesn't want to have one with you. This can become an obsessive thing where we end up frustrated, disillusioned, and humiliated. We read about it, in its worst forms, in news accounts of obsessed fans who stalk celebrities dreaming of becoming the celebs' best buddies. For most people it doesn't go that far. But in truth, most of us have petted piranhas in less virulent ways—and have ended up the worse for it. And in the process we have blindly ignored other relationships that were ours for the taking.

As I write this I'm thinking of a particular speaking opportunity. For years, I felt that I had something to offer the listeners, and certainly at least as much as some of the other invited speakers. But no invitation came, so I became somewhat troubled. Had I offended someone? Did the host not like me? I played many scenarios over in my mind. Finally, I came to terms with the situation, and here are several principles that have helped me cope.

First, I've had to admit a hard truth to myself. This was more about *my* ego than anything else. What was I hoping that an invitation to this venue would prove or validate in my life? After all, if I'm sincerely trying to reflect and minister for Jesus, why not simply trust him to fill my calendar? My value comes from God—period, end of sentence.

Second, I decided to go out of my way to be kind to the host involved. When I have an opportunity to hear him speak, I attend. I go out of my way to speak cordially to him. Then, after the event, I usually send him a handwritten note of thanks. So far he has never responded. At first that bugged me too. But again, I had to question my own motives. Was I simply trying to curry his favor—still hoping for that elusive invitation? Or was I being sincere—attending in order to learn something worthwhile and graciously thanking him for his insights?

This has helped me accept the truth that not everyone is going to like me. It's not necessarily my fault—or theirs. The fact is, some people have better chemistry than others. That's not good or bad. That's just the way things are. For me, a pleaser, that's a hard truth. But as I've come to accept it, life has become better. It was Jesus who reminded us "that the truth shall set you free."

Life is too short to pet piranhas—because you'll never make a friend doing so. And you're likely to come up missing a couple of fingers in the process. Likewise, life is also too short to chase people who don't want to be caught. There are always lots of other fish out there. Frequently, these are the ones we notice the least. But they may be the ones with the highest FQ (friendship quotient.) Truly mutual friendships are the only really good ones.

Why climb to the highest limb when there's a big, red, ripe apple at shoulder level?

29

LOOK FOR THE SPOTS

B lind spots. Even people who have conquered many of their personal demons and have blessed multitudes have blind spots. I suppose it's part of what makes humans, well, human.

Yesterday a friend shared a sad story about another man who is losing his marriage. In the conversation, my friend explained how both of them had worked for one of the best known evangelists in America. This evangelist has become internationally famous. His books have sold millions of copies. And he's appeared on all of the important TV shows. My friend explained that in the early days of his ministry, the evangelist had had the tender heart of a pastor. And to this day he still has a gentle, giving side. But as he became more famous, he became less vigilant. The ministry became increasingly more focused on him. Others noticed this, and in his better moments, even he realized the problem. My friend first went to work for this Christian leader because, as he put it, "I already have too many 'yes' men and I need someone who will hold me accountable." Trouble is, when my friend fulfilled his job description, his employment soon ended. Despite all of his good traits, this man of God has some huge blind spots.

Here's my question: Do we see spots? By that, I mean are we constantly searching our hearts and motives? Or do we choose to believe all the good others may say about us—and ignore the negative? Are we willing to look deeply and deal with our shortcomings—or do we deny, deflect, and disagree when others dare to point them out?

The Bible tells us that God "rebukes and chastens" his children. And I am grateful that he does. But the truth is, as one whom he has taken to the woodshed on many occasions, I don't like it. It's painful. It's embarrassing. It's lonely. Some years ago, it finally occurred to me that maybe there's a way to avoid some of God's chastisement. Could it be that God works like we human fathers work? If they forced me to do so, I was always willing to rebuke, chasten, and punish my own kids. I did the hard stuff to help them avoid even more painful predicaments in the future. But I never enjoyed it. "So," I wondered, "could it not follow that God would prefer not to punish me either?" That led to the next question, "How do I avoid God's chastisement?" Boing! The light bulb finally came on. Maybe if I behave better, God won't have to discipline me so often. But to behave better, I must first see my errors. To do that I need to be searching for my blind spots just like windshield wipers continually remove the rain from the pane.

As one who spends less time in God's woodshed than I used to, let me share some insights that I have found helpful.

1. Listen to your Father. One of the things God's Spirit does is convict us of our sins. Awareness of our blind spots tends to come more readily when one is open and listening to God's promptings in our heart. I'm learning that God prefers to tap me on the shoulder. He only grabs the switch when I don't pay attention to his nudging.

2. Listen to your critics. Now this is a tricky one. I'm not suggesting that you take out a note pad for everyone who wants to give you a list of criticisms. Healthy living requires a thick skin. But spiritual health also requires that we maintain a tender heart. We need people in our lives who will help us stay alert to good behavior. These are trusted friends or mentors who have our

best interest at heart, but don't hesitate to grab us by the ears, nail our tongue to the floor, and get in our face when we've blown it. The minister I cited above would be better for it if he'd followed through this way with my friend.

3. Try hard to have "out-of-body" experiences. In other words, try to see yourself as others do. Is your behavior towards others the sort of behavior that would ingratiate yourself to you?

Life is too short *not* to see the blind spots in your own life for three reasons. First, it will make you a more likable person. Second, it will keep you too busy to worry so much about the misdeeds and slights from others. Thirdly, it will cause your Father to smile.

30

DEMONSTRATE CHARACTER WHEN THE GOING GETS TOUGH

2008 was a lousy year for the economy. Particularly hard hit was the U.S. airline industry. It had been seven years since the vicious attacks on the World Trade Center in New York and the Pentagon in Washington D.C. However, the airline business had still not fully recovered from loses it had suffered for the next couple of years, as many Americans were simply afraid to fly. During that period, the industry lost billions of dollars. Compounding matters was the fact that, by 2008, oil prices had shot through the roof. While we were paying over $4.00 per gallon for gasoline, the cost of crude tipped $160 a barrel. Suddenly the airlines were taking it on the chin again. While possible to operate profitably with crude at $85, maybe even $100, a barrel, these new, never-seen-before prices were mind jarring.

Like the other airlines, AMR (the parent company of American Airlines) for years had fought one dragon after another. Then to add insult to injury, a terribly unfair ruling by the Federal Aviation Administration dealt another costly blow to this company in 2008. In what I believe to be one of the most outrageous decisions a government bureaucracy has ever made, the FAA grounded nearly half of American's fleet because of a minor wiring issue that had nothing to do with passenger safety, according to a number of industry observers. During those horrible days the company lost millions of dollars—all at the very moment that fuel prices were skyrocketing. Passengers, not knowing the facts, blamed the airline. All over the country gate agents and flight employees stoically smiled and apologized to inconvenienced passengers for something that was not their fault—and was costing them dearly.

Over the years all five of the other major legacy carriers have filed bankruptcy in one form or another. But American has steadfastly refused to follow the trend. Instead, they watched as other companies sometimes walked away from financial obligations to venders and employees—essentially shrugging their collective shoulders and saying, "Too bad."

Why didn't American Airlines do what their competitors had done? There were all sorts of ways to rationalize a bankruptcy. And imagine how tough it was to watch some of their competitors emerge from bankruptcy (no longer legally liable for their original commitments) now able to offer their customers perks that American was hard pressed to match. Another important note: Through these tough days American has never stopped paying into its employees' pension fund either. So again I ask, why didn't American just follow the trend?

I have it on a good source that, while it was discussed in top level meetings at the company's Dallas headquarters, there were a number of executives who simply had a moral problem with the entire notion. In a personal conversation with one of the company's high-level managers, I learned how the airline's executive suite has struggled to take the moral highroad even when they could have saved money by cutting corners. Yet through it all, AMR has elected to do the right thing. Under the leadership of Gerard Arpey, the company has fought staggering headwinds. Not all the employees have agreed with his decisions, but over the years he has built a culture of openness and honesty. As an honest broker, Arpey and his team have slain dragons to maintain a solid coalition of customers, shareholders, and employees.

As individuals, we can learn a lot from the corporate world. Moral corporate cultures are not the product of random, do-whatever-it-takes business models. Morality in a business is the product of morality in the executive suite. In turn, that moral compass is reflected down line. Sound old fashioned? Maybe. But that is the way AMR sees things.

So what are the personal take-aways for us in all of this? I'm glad you asked.

1. To rephrase an overworked cliché, I would suggest that when the tough get going, its good advice to stand back, watch, and learn. You're likely to find that you are not the only one who is trying to do the right thing.
2. Be a cheerleader. When you see someone else (or in this case, a company) doing the right thing, make a big deal about it. Tell your friends. Compliment the person or company. And vote with your dollars. Do business with those who are doing right.
3. Pray for them. There really is a spiritual battle going on. "For our struggle is not against flesh and blood, but against the rulers, against the authorities, against the powers of this dark world and against the spiritual forces of evil in the heavenly realms" (Ephesians 6:12, NIV). We need to be aggressively promoting and praying that good will win over evil.

Anytime we see anyone holding the torch high in this dark world, it is a challenge for us to stand shoulder to shoulder. Life is too short not to take a stand.

31

HELP MEET THE NEEDS OF OTHERS

For much of my religious life, I was frustrated. I knew that, as a Christian, I was supposed to share my faith. But on balance, it was not a particularly rewarding experience. My mode of operation was basically to get some poor soul in my crosshairs and try to sit him down long enough for me explain how he was wrong. Then, with phase one accomplished, I'd baptize him into Jesus. But there was a problem with this. It's what salespeople call "buyer's remorse." More often than not, within a few months, he had lost interest—and was nowhere to be found.

In more recent years it has occurred to me that Jesus didn't evangelize that way. Jesus was never in a hurry. For him, conversion wasn't about "closing" another sale. And it wasn't to make him feel more spiritual. As a matter of fact, Matthew records some of Jesus' last instructions to his disciples this way: "As you go about whatever else you're doing always be ready to share the good news of what I've done in your lives" (loosely paraphrased from Matthew 28).

For Jesus, seeing a lost person turn her heart to him was about that individual. Jesus understood that people are not robots who can be force fed a stack of facts and, then, immediately and predictably come to his inevitable conclusion. Instead, having made humankind in his own image, Jesus realized that people are all about relationship. We thrive on relationship. We find our joy in relationship.

The Jesus approach was to first find a person's perceived need and tend to it. He fed hungry people. He healed sick people. He befriended lonely people. He picked up the scraps of humanity and invested himself in their lives by meeting their needs. Then, with a solid bridge of relationship constructed, he shared the good news. Some years later, the Apostle Paul mused, "How beautiful are the feet of the one who brings the good news."

So with this as my springboard, allow me to share an idea that you might want to try. Begin by selecting a restaurant near your home. For me, this will probably be a nearby Waffle House. I won't digress too far here, but I want to explain why I mention the Waffle House. If you're not a Southerner, you may not be familiar with these delightful greasy spoons that dot our part of the country. While they're certainly not known for health-conscious menus, there's nothing better than one of their famous waffles. But there's another, more practical, reason why I prefer Waffle Houses for this particular ministry. I call Waffle Houses "cave torches." These 24/7 diners are built with huge glass windows and filled with bright, fluorescent lighting. At night, they look like torches in a cave. (Stay with me here. In a moment you'll see why this is important.)

Since it may take several attempts to find the "right" situation, an especially good time of year to begin this project might be about mid-November. Go into your selected restaurant as often as it takes to meet a server who obviously is hurting. Maybe it will be a young woman wearing a button with a picture of two toddlers. A second glance tells you that she isn't wearing a wedding band. You can pretty well fill in the blanks. Gradually, over a couple of visits, you begin a dialogue with her. Then one day simply ask, "I'm going to say a prayer for my meal in a moment. Is there anything I can pray about for you?" Whether she accepts or rejects your offer, your warmth will likely touch her soul. Don't rush. Simply continue visiting the restaurant and always be sure to sit in her station. Talk. Communicate. Show true concern.

Then, as Christmas draws closer, think about this young woman. Ask yourself, "What does she need that she probably doesn't already have?" Note: This is not the time to over-spiritualize things and declare to yourself, "She needs Jesus!" Sure she does. You know that. The trouble is, she is still probably unaware of her true need. But she does perceive the need for enough money to buy some toys for her kids.

So before your next visit (now just a few days prior to Christmas), gather the family together and agree not to buy another bunch of idiot gifts that no one really wants or needs. Instead, determine that *this* Christmas will be for Jesus—and the girl at the restaurant. That evening go back to the restaurant. Order a meal and visit a little more. By this time, your server may be looking forward to your visits. Spend a couple of extra moments and inquire about her children. Talk about anything she wants to discuss. Remind her that she'll be in your prayers, and wish her the merriest Christmas ever. Then, as you leave, slip a $100 bill under your plate. Quietly go out to your car—and watch her pick the plate up. That, dear one, is Christmas! (By the way, this is why I prefer restaurants with big windows and lots of light.)

When the New Year turns, drop back in. Don't make any big deal—just be your friendly self. In time, the odds are high she will open her heart and soul to you. That's when it becomes person to personal. Then, as her true friend, you can begin to share the *really* good news. Isn't life too short not to do it the Jesus way?

32

BE REAL

N aming this chapter has been a challenge. I considered various titles like, "Take Your Clothes Off," or "Get Naked." Granted, such labels would have been real attention grabbers, but they would probably also have been too provocative. Since my goal here is to communicate, not titillate, I opted for the tamer title above. But don't confuse my more puritanical heading for a lack of passion. What I want to discuss in this visit is a key to effective spiritual living that most of us never understand or apply.

Simply put, when another person trusts you enough to seek your advice, or especially to confess a sin in their life, it is a great honor. But it also presents you with a serious dilemma. One approach is to sit back stoically like a priest in a box. And, without even intending to so, you can communicate an air of spiritual superiority that makes the one confessing feel smaller and less worthy with each word he utters. Frankly, this is my preferred method of operation. It makes the whole experience much easier for me. Everything is non-personal and, well, clinical. I go away with virtually no spent emotional energy. But sadly, the poor soul on the other side of the table frequently leaves feeling even worse and more defeated than he did prior to his privileged visit with me. My silence has spoken volumes. He leaves convinced that I am a decid-edly better person than the facts warrant. I leave the meeting with my piety intact—feeling pretty good, but he feels spiritually humiliated and naked.

The other approach is far more difficult, but in some cases it is absolutely the right thing to do. It requires that we, in essence, remove our spiritual clothing so the other person doesn't feel so alone and embarrassed. In this scenario I must come clean by admitting my own filth and that I too struggle with similar sins. This is when I look at the person who is baring his soul to me and I say, "Jason, I love you, brother. You and I have traveled the same road. I have been trapped in that same (or name a similar) sin myself. I know how you feel." Those are powerful words, and they are hard to say. But by saying them, we level the playing field and, once again, realize that we are all on the same footing before God. We are all sinners. My sins are no better or worse than yours. We are all at eye level—one with the other. The only difference between people is that some have accepted God and experienced his saving grace, and others haven't.

In the Bible, James shared some advice with the young church that is still as contemporary as today's headlines. He told his Christian friends that they should confess their sins to one another and pray for one another. How refreshing. How egalitarian. There is no hierarchy here, just sinners who desperately need the touch of the Master's hand.

James concludes his direction with the promise that the prayer of a "righteous man avails much." Have you ever wondered what he meant by the words "avails much?" Could it be that it is much more than we will ever see or know until we stand before God's throne and see the faces of others who stand with us there because we stood with them here?

33

BE SLOW TO
CRITICIZE THE
BELIEFS OF OTHERS

We've all heard the phrase, "Majoring on the minors." This is sometimes said when attempting to describe a person who wastes time on the unimportant and ignores the most important. It's like going to a movie and leaving after the previews. When you think about it, many of life's greatest problems, worst failures, and most painful defeats come when we sacrifice the significant for the shiny—the eternal for the temporal. This is an important concept to consider in a book like this, because mislabeling can result in totally missing the big picture.

Last week I was visiting with a group of church leaders. These were all good-hearted men. But I was taken aback when one of them blurted out, "We're a conservative church."

This unexpected comment piqued my curiosity, so I inquired, "What do you mean by 'conservative'?"

"It means we don't do any hand clapping during the worship service," came his response.

I wish I could tell you that I was surprised, but I wasn't. Having visited in hundreds of churches around the world, I've seen, heard, and been exposed to a lot of stuff. Very little surprises me anymore.

However, my travels have led me to believe that when we mislabel, we do it to our own hurt. Often our mislabeling works against our very purpose of trying to reach other strugglers who have not yet found our Jesus. Sometimes this makes me mad. It always makes me sad.

We have so butchered the words "conservative" and "liberal" that many of us wouldn't know either if we met one. Before I go further, let me be crystal clear about a few things. I am a conservative. Socially, politically, and religiously—I'm right of Attila the Hun on most issues! But I refuse to allow others to highjack the vocabulary and insist that I misuse the word "conservative." Being conservative has nothing to do with which translation of the Bible one selects. It doesn't involve whether one's church has a praise team, a choir, or sings traditional hymns. And it certainly has zero to do with whether or not I clap during worship. By contrast, a person isn't necessarily a liberal simply because she claps her hands, reads from another translation, or prefers different music.

Religiously speaking a conservative is someone who accepts the Bible at face value, believes in the deity of Christ, and holds to the historic, orthodox views of Christianity. A liberal is, by contrast, one who questions Jesus' rightful place in the Godhead, or denies the inspiration of the Scripture, or suggests that Jesus is less than the only way to God.

Since many of my readers are in the conservative camp, what I have to say here will be aimed at you. You are not a conservative (a good thing) simply because you are a traditionalist (potentially a good or a bad thing.) But one thing is certain: Being a traditionalist instantly becomes a bad thing when the traditions you espouse begin to replace the bedrock issues of the Christian faith.

Being conservative involves a doggedly steadfast allegiance (devotion) to Jesus and to Jesus alone. We need to always be vigilant—aggressively cutting off the baggage of legalism, which in itself can *become* our religion. This was the thrust of much of Jesus' ministry. Jesus rarely became provoked with "pedestrian" sinners who were desperate people fully aware of their brokenness and failed lives. But with those who should have been mature believers—but used their religion as a clock for legalism, hypocrisy, and self-righteousness—he took no prisoners. Mark tells a story about one such confrontation. It happened one day when Jesus was confronted by some Jewish Pharisees in Jerusalem (these are the traditionalists in this story). The Pharisees, who were jealous that more and more people were leaving them to follow Jesus, chided Jesus for allowing his disciples to eat without washing their hands properly. Jesus, always one to see the big picture, unloaded on them:

> Isaiah was right when he prophesied about you hypocrites; as it is written: 'These people honor me with their lips, but their hearts are far from me. They worship me in vain; their teachings are but rules taught by men.' You have let go of the commands of God and are holding on to the traditions of men . . . You have a fine way of setting aside the commands of God in order to observe your own traditions!" (7:6-9, NIV)

The next time someone criticizes you (or you're tempted to criticize someone else) for not coming up to some perceived bar of spirituality, go slowly. Be sure that the criticism is founded on clear, biblical teaching—and not simply someone's opinion. Learn the difference between being a conservative and being a traditionalist. Remember, a lot of religion is mislabeled.

34

GIVE GRACE TO ALL

I was six years old when Superman died. By the 1950s, George Reeves had become the human personification of the DC Comic book hero. He starred in over one hundred television episodes as the real life Man of Steel. I still remember watching him. He was glorious and inspiring. I wanted to be just like Superman. When a cereal company offered a Superman belt as a premium for sending in enough box-tops (and probably some cash), I became a cereal eating machine. When my shiny red belt arrived in the mail, I promptly put it on and jumped off a platform convinced that I could fly. The myth was beginning to melt.

As it turned out, Superman wasn't faster than a speeding bullet. In the early morning hours of June 16, 1959, George Reeves (a.k.a. Superman) was found dead in his Benedict Canyon home in Los Angeles. It is generally thought that the gunshot wound to his head was self-inflicted. Those were dark days for young boys across the nation. "How could Superman die?" they wondered. As parents dutifully tried to protect youngsters from the gory details, the fact remained: Superman was gone.

Have you ever had a hero? Have you ever been disappointed by that hero? Possibly your hero wasn't a fictionalized champion. Maybe he or she was a person you had grown to esteem and respect. If you were young, you may have wanted to "be just like her" when you grew up. If you met your hero as an adult, maybe you copied his mannerisms and strove to behave like he behaved. Then one day you saw him do or say something that didn't fit. At first you tried to ignore it. Then you tried to explain it away. Finally, you admitted to yourself that he wasn't who or what you had thought. You felt disillusioned and betrayed. You may have assured yourself, "I'll never do that again—no one is dependable." And in your hasty retreat, you lost more than you gained. One day you awoke to realize that you no longer trusted yourself to trust others.

The trouble with having heroes is that we build them up to the point that when they finally act human, we're crestfallen. Here are the hard, cold facts:

1. Hero worship is dangerous. It is a shortcut to bitterness and cynicism. God never intended for us to have more than one God. That's why he warned that we should have "no other gods" before him. There's a fine line between rightful admiration and destructive "person worship." Watch for that line.

2. Don't expect humans to be more than . . . human. The greatest heroes of history have all fallen at one time or another. Abraham, the father of the Jewish nation, was a coward and a liar. On two occasions he claimed that his wife was his sister—to keep his own fat out of the fire with a couple of amorous kings who had their eyes on Sarah. Moses was the man whom God chose to deliver the Ten Commandments to the Jews. But Moses also dishonored God by publicly disobeying him. James and John, two of Jesus' apostles, lobbied to murder an entire town that they were mad at. And other stories, as contemporary as today's headlines, abound of preachers, priests, and politicians who knew to do better—but chose to do worse.

3. The devil is smart. Why should he waste his time on a minnow when he can catch a whale? Doesn't it make logical sense that Satan would far rather bring down a high-profile hero than someone like you or me? He understands the domino effect. By

knocking a high-profile saint to his knees, many lesser saints (whose eyes were on the man of God rather than God himself) will also fall.

4. Allow grace to all humans. When someone you love or admire stumbles, pray for him. Be in a hurry to forgive. Over the years, I've watched people whom I knew and admired who made a lot of money, blockbuster movies, and gold records do some very ungodly things. Among my friends are high profile Christians who have served prison and jail time for drug abuse, white collar crime, and attempting to have sex with underage boys.

What I must remember is that it's dangerous for me to look up to (or down at) any other human being. All of us have fallen short of God's expectation for us. In God's economy, all sins are equal. The human side of me resists and rejects this notion. But it's true. James tells us that, even if we don't fall into other sins, the ones we do commit make us equally guilty before God. Jesus said if I hope to be forgiven of my sins I must be ready, willing, and eager to forgive others. This includes those I've put on pedestals.

35

BE AGGRESSIVE IN YOUR SEARCH FOR GOD'S HEART

I have led a most blessed life. If I die before this chapter is complete, that's okay. It's been a ball! Sure there have been plenty of disappointments and struggles. But all in all, things have been really good.

I'm convinced that much of the joy that I've known is directly traceable to those early memories of sitting on Mom's lap and hearing about Jesus. Before I was born, Mother determined that Jesus would be on the front burner of my young life. She stopped her job as a teacher in the Oak Ridge school system so she could raise me by word and example. Long before the WWJD (What Would Jesus Do?) bracelets were even thought of, Mom was pointing to Jesus as the guide for my young life. The day wasn't finished until Mom had read a Bible story. And the night light was never extinguished until we had said our prayers.

With this as my "life springboard," it will come as no surprise that I have a high regard today for the Bible. The Hebrew writer tells us that God's word "is living and active and sharper than any two-edged sword . . . ." Over the years, there have been plenty of times when I thought I pretty well had a handle on all that God had to tell me. And each time, God has shown me how wrong I was. Today, I am at a point in life where I wait expectantly for more insights from his word. It is always amazing how—sometimes when I am reading it for the tenth, or the fiftieth, or the hundredth time—God opens my mind to a new vista of meaning in a passage which I *thought* I had already fully explored. Sometimes these "boing moments" are heartening, and sometimes they are challenging. Let me share one which God has just used to open my eyes a bit further.

There is a passage that says that God referred to King David as "a man after my own heart, who will do all my will" (Acts 13:22b, NASB; see also 1 Samuel 13:14). Maybe you have heard this short passage read and repeated by others all of your life. Possibly you have heard sermons preached on it and seen books written about it. Frankly, I have believed for years that I "got it." I thought I fully understood this passage. Had you asked me even a day ago to explain this verse to you I would have said something like, "It means that King David was a man who thought like, and sought for, God. His worldview reflected God's worldview. He strove to be God's man."

I still believe all of that to be true. But just this afternoon, God opened my eyes to a different (yet complimentary) angle from which to view this passage. See if this makes sense to you, too.

Is it possible that this comment about David (recorded more than a thousand years after his death by Luke) has an even deeper and more profound meaning? I wonder if we should put the greatest emphasis on the word "after"? What if this is not a statement about the passive nature of David who simply reflected God's way of thinking? What if it also speaks to the aggressive way that King David chased *after* God—forcefully fighting to hear, and become more like, God? Could it be that David was chasing after God the way a guy chases a girl whom he absolutely *must* meet? I wonder if David was so enamored by God that God had become his "great obsession." No matter what got in his way, he remained focused on his goal of reaching deeply into God and taking hold of God's heart. If this is true, then it adds greater meaning to the last words from the above passage. God concludes by saying that David is a man "who will do *all* my will." Just like a guy who is trying to woo his dream girl, David was anxious to do anything that God willed.

Maybe I'm dead wrong. Possibly these are just the musings of a guy with too much time on his hands. But I don't think so. Wouldn't I be the better for it to become more aggressive in my search for God's heart? What if I was willing to knock down walls to get closer to God? What if I began every morning by putting on my spiritual running shoes determined to spend that day chasing *after* my God?

36

GET ENOUGH REST

S ounds pretty straight and simple, right? It is. This is exactly what our moms told us when we were six. But in fact, a high percentage of Americans live their entire adulthoods with chronic sleep deprivation. Many of these people know that something is wrong—but never really figure it out.

We all have heard of kids going to sleep during finals week. And we've all seen the news accounts of drivers who have dozed off into oncoming traffic. But I would suggest that the majority of harm from sleep deprivation is the part of the iceberg that's below the waterline. A combined university study in 2007 revealed that lack of sleep can cause individuals to become incapable of correctly accessing and dealing with emotional events. It is generally believed that sleep deprivation can be a contributor to a host of maladies, including mood swings, heart disease, certain cancers, bi-polar disorder, weight gain, depression, and even suicide. One study indicated that there was a forty percent increase in depression and thirty percent more suicidal thoughts among sleep deprived teenagers.

One of the simplest, cheapest, and least painful ways we have to maintain good physical, mental, and spiritual health is to get enough rest. Now if you are a Type A, or a pleaser, or a young mom, you're probably saying, "Sure. That's easy for you to say. You don't know the stresses I live with."

My response would be twofold. First, I am a Type A and a pleaser (but admittedly, thus far not a mom). I know how it feels to spend life on a treadmill.

And second, your very response proves my point. To become irritated at what you know to be correct and truthful advice often is not the response of a happy, well-adjusted person. It is the sort of moody malaise of someone who needs her sleep.

I remember a young woman who has recently dealt with (and conquered) a bout of depression. She is very intelligent. She is devout (a children's minister.) She is well educated. During those difficult months, she got good counseling and the proper medications. But I remember a breakthrough conversation that she and I shared. One day it hit me—she wasn't getting enough rest. This young lady loved to stay up late and sleep in late. The trouble was, while she could (and did) stay up too late, her job forced her to get up early. We both realized that there was a direct relationship between her mood and how much sleep she was getting. While I'm most thankful for the psychiatric help she received, I'm convinced that her improved sleep discipline also made a huge difference.

Think back. Don't forget that Jesus' calendar was loaded while he was on earth. There he was with approximately one thousand days to minister! During those three years, it was do-or-die. There was no room for error on this mission. Jesus had to communicate the gospel message and establish a beachhead from which to spread his eternal story after he returned to heaven. Had it been me, I would have worked hundred-hour weeks. No vacations. No time off. But that wasn't how Jesus did it. He always took time to recharge his batteries. Jesus knew better than any mortal how critical his mission was. There was no time for depression, poor judgment, or bad decisions. He had to be at his best all the time. So, isn't it interesting how Jesus always found time to rest?

And he was apparently a pretty sound sleeper, too. Do you recall the night that the storm blew up on the Sea of Galilee? Although some of them were professional fishermen, his apostles panicked. They were convinced that the boat was about to end up on the sea bottom. Yet, despite the storm's winds and waves, Jesus slept soundly on until awakened by his guys.

If you are sincere and passionate about what you do, get enough sleep to do it well. This means learning to draw the line. If you know you must get up early (which, as I'll discuss in our next visit, is usually a good discipline in its own right), then turn off the TV, say "good night" to your friends—and go to bed on time.

Don't fret; I don't intend to tell you how much sleep you should get. There are two reasons for this. One, I'm not a medical expert. But two, I am smart enough to know that there is no one-size-fits-all on this topic. I have known a few people who can do well for years with only four or five hours of sleep nightly. A few, at the other end of the continuum, seem to need ten or more hours of sleep to perform at their peak. For me, it seems to be about six to seven hours. I'm not trying to micro manage your life, but simply attempting to share some broad principles that I will trust you to fine tune.

Remember, life is too short not to live it with all the gusto we can muster. Rested people do more, they do it better, and they certainly enjoy the journey the most.

37

START EARLY
AND MOVE SLOWLY

I really believe that. I'm convinced that snooze buttons on alarm clocks reinforce bad behavior, and do more harm than good. A snooze button allows me to do something in the morning (when my will power is at its lowest) that I promised myself I wouldn't do last night (when I was thinking clearly.) So it's important to come up with a strategy to get up and get going on time.

I still remember the summer of 1970. I had just graduated from high school and had decided to spend that last summer before college selling Bibles door-to-door for the Southwestern Company. Their plan was simple: Knock on your first door at 8:00 am every morning. To do that I had to get up early, eat breakfast, plan my day, and drive (or peddle) to the location of that first door. As an adult, none of this sounds too difficult. But for a seventeen-year-old kid who'd never been away from home—much less living in a boarding house in another state with another equally under-motivated buddy—it was quiet a stretch! As you might imagine, my buddy Dave and I were snooze button-aholics. So we decided to conquer our little dilemma with a financial incentive. At night we'd position the alarm clock across the room from the bed. As we set it for wake-up time, we each put a $20 bill under the clock. Then, in the morning, whoever turned it off first got both $20's. Talk about motivated teens, we found ourselves waking up early waiting for the clock to ring!

In the previous chapter, I made the case for getting enough sleep. Now is when I bring some balance to the picture and say, "Enough is enough! Get up and get going." Many of your day's most important matters can be best prayed over, read through, and mediated about in the early part of the day. But like most things that are good for us, we tend to avoid this one, too. So let me share a few thoughts that may persuade you to give this life-skill a try.

Remember that Jesus set the example for us here. On a number of occasions we read about Jesus getting up early in the morning. Mark mentions one of those times: "Very early in the morning, while it was still dark, Jesus got up, left the house and went off to a solitary place, where he prayed" (1:35, NIV). Maybe Jesus realized some important things that we need to take note of. Often the early morning hours are the only "quiet time" of the day. This is before the appointments start. It's before the phone begins to ring. It's before one kid is pulling the other kid's hair. It's before the "noise" of the world starts to happen.

In my own experience, I've noticed that I often tend to be more creative in the early morning. During the twenty-plus years that I headed an ad agency, these first hours of the day were when I conceived some of our best campaigns. I have two favorite "ponder places." One is actually in my bed. Sometimes, provided I wake up early enough, I lie in bed (maybe half asleep) and think. Lots of good ideas have occurred to me in this "ponder place." My other favorite "ponder place" is the shower. (Now, if you're a strict conservationist, this is going to irritate you.) I love to take long showers in the morning and simply think. Yesterday morning I was in my hydro "ponder place" thinking. Finally, with three important ideas bubbling in my brain, I burst out of the shower into the bedroom where I stood dripping as I furiously wrote notes before I forgot anything. (Note to self: Consider keeping a notepad closer to the shower.)

As a matter of fact, I'm writing a significant portion of this chapter on a Sunday morning. It's fairly early and I'm already busy putting this to paper. My creative juices are flowing. Since I'm in a hotel, there will be the mundane issues of pressing a wrinkled shirt and jacket. I will also have time to read my Bible. And since I'm due to teach and preach this morning, I'll have time to do some vocal exercises by getting up early. These are all things that I don't have the time to do on equivalent Sunday's when I jump out of bed barely in time to get to church. Frankly, I like this morning better. Getting up early is a good thing.

Footnote: Like anything else, this good idea can be taken to unhealthy extremes. If you're a workaholic (I'm a recovering workaholic myself), don't use this as an excuse to do even more. For a number of years I crawled out of bed way too early way too often.

Be kind to yourself. Learn to do what one famous (and very skinny) singer did. Although he ate lightly almost all the time, there was one day a week when he allowed himself "comfort food." He and his family ate whatever they wished. (I understand KFC was a favorite.) In the same way, allow yourself some "comfort sleep." If getting up early isn't your cup of tea, be moderate. Get up less early. Select one day per week as your "comfort sleep" day and leave the shades down until ten o'clock.

Remember, your purpose for getting up early isn't to load more into your wagon. It's to allow you to start more slowly and deliberately. Drink a cup of coffee and watch the sun rise. Read a couple of chapters in that novel. Prepare a handwritten note. Re-listen to a CD of last Sunday's sermon. Talk to God. And listen to him talk to you. Be at peace.

38

LEARN WHAT
TRUE PEACE IS

One of the most insightful men I know is Colonel Michael Whittington, a retired United States Air Force Command Chaplain. Recently, I heard Whit (that's what his friends call him) tell a story that went back to when he was working on his doctorate. The grueling combination of hours of studies along with a fulltime job, plus his duties as a young husband and father, had led him to ask his lead professor to pray with him. As the two men kneeled together, Whit pled, "God remove my struggles."

His professor promptly jumped to his feet in the middle of the prayer and said, "Whit, whatever you do, don't pray that God will remove your struggles. He might grant your request!"

Wow, what was that about? What was wrong with asking God to remove his struggles? After all, wouldn't a struggle-free life also be a much more enjoyable life? Accepting this line of reasoning I, too, have prayed for this same release from pain and struggle hundreds of times. But today, with the benefit of hindsight, I think I know why Whit's professor responded as he did.

The fact is: Peace is not a lack of struggle. Peace is seeing God *in* that struggle.

Struggle is inevitable. Maybe your immediate response to that statement is, "Tell me about it! I'm up to my ears in grief and problems right now. Frankly, I'm not sure how much longer I can hold on."

If you aren't currently in the midst of struggle, one is coming. Last night, as I lay in bed, I found myself thanking God for his blessings. At the moment, things in the Diggs' household are sailing along pretty well. Bonnie and I are contented empty nesters. All four kids are healthy, happy, and in love with Jesus. Two are joyfully married to their best friends—and our third child just became engaged five nights ago. The fourth is in college making good grades and even better friends. And we all seem to be relatively healthy. But as I prayed I became aware that, while praise was appropriate, the future also holds struggles. It will be in those moments that I will need the strong hand of God to hold my head above the waters. My human side fears and resists this notion. But it is inescapable, inevitable—and even good.

More often than not, my walk with God grows most in the midst of struggle. That may be an indictment of my own miniscule faith, but it's the truth. An unhappy child, an argument with Bonnie, a Christian who selects me to be his punching bag, a disappointing conversation with one of my doctors—all of these things force me back to God. It's when my breath has been knocked out that I tend to breathe in God's inspiration most deeply. When I'm emotionally parched that's when his living water tastes the best.

The darker the cave, the more brightly his light shines. These are times when I find myself in deeper prayer. These are days when I realize my desperate need for God's touch. These are periods when I tend to have more empathy for others who are themselves hurting. These are times when I must decide whether my Christianity is real or fake.

Several years ago I began a ministry to teach God's kids how to use God's money God's way. The basic message was to trust God to provide for our financial and material needs. Frankly, in hindsight, I realize that I was far too removed from many of the people to whom I was attempting to minister. But my own economic storm was on the way.

After the storm had passed, one day Bonnie looked at me and said, "Steve, I don't think you would be able to minister as effectively today to people who are suffering with money problems if we had not gone through that painful situation ourselves." I couldn't reject her rationale. I had to admit that that most difficult experience had taught me some important life lessons that have helped me to empathize more deeply with the people I am attempting to help.

That experience was painful and embarrassing. But I am learning to agree with James who boldly reminded us: "Consider it pure joy, my brothers, whenever you face trials of many kinds, because you know that the testing of your faith develops perseverance. Perseverance must finish its work so that you may be mature and complete, not lacking anything" (James 1:2-4, NIV).

When it's all said and done, short periods of pain, if used correctly, can render long periods of gain. In a world that is fixated on the here and now, it's important to develop an appreciation for the painful events that can make us better people—and more able to touch others around us who are hurting. The trick is learning to see the eternal in the temporal, and realizing that life is too short to miss this bigger picture.

39

CHOOSE WHERE TO PUT YOUR FAITH

I spent a lot of my life believing that I knew far more than I did. Today, in my fifties, I'm continually amazed at how stone stupid I am. A lot of the quick-fix, pre-fab answers that I used to flippantly throw out to others don't work for me anymore. I cannot tell you why there is suffering. I'm not sure why God doesn't always respond to my prayers with clear, lightning bolt answers. And I'm still curious to know where Cain found his wife.

But these things I do know: God is real. He is there. And he cares.

So again, I ask, why doesn't God reveal himself to me the way *I* want him to? Why do his followers get hurt? Why can't we "prove" God? Why do smart people reject him? Do they know something that I don't? Let me take on some of these questions and share some thoughts that may help you see the bigger picture.

To begin, I believe God is real. But what do I say to those who claim that he doesn't exist? Maybe it is as simple as repeating the same question over and over. When an atheist makes his case that we evolved from a lower species, our question should always be, "Where did that come from?" Eventually, you will witness a confounded atheist. Because at some point he must admit that he doesn't have an answer. Maybe his moment of frustration will register when he points to single-cell animals, or the primordial soup they came from, or cross-pollination from another planet—and you ask one more time, "Where did that come from?" At this moment you both know it—he's stuck. All he can logically do is admit that, based on his own line of reasoning, he accepts the concept of spontaneous generation. (This is the idea that something *can* come from nothing.) In that moment, the only remaining question is, which is more logical: The belief that something can suddenly pop into existence where absolutely nothing exists; or that there is such a thing as an eternal Creator who made it all happen? For my money, it is far more logical and requires far less faith to accept the latter than it does the former.

So why do so many educated people deny God's existence? Why do atheist disbelieve? You may wonder, "Do they know something that I don't know?" Maybe it has less to do with the cerebral than it does with the nature of humans. By nature, we humans want to be our own gods. The boys and girls with the stellar IQs deny God for the same reason people whose IQs start with a decimal point deny God. Granted, the eggheads are more articulate and intimidating—but at its root, all atheists have one thing in common: They want to be their own gods. Why? Because to admit that there *is* a God leads to a next (and most uncomfortable) question, "What does this God expect of me?"

You see, to admit that there is a God is to admit that we are not at the top of the food chain. And primal though it be, all of us fear someone who holds our destiny in his hands. That's why we speak politely to bosses we don't respect. That's why we check the speedometer when we pass a policeman. That's why we take a phone call from an important client when we're on a family fishing trip.

As to why God doesn't reveal more to us than he does, I don't know. Why do Christians suffer along with everyone else? There may be three things at play here.

First, how different do you suspect things would be if people got a "get out of jail free" card the instant they became Christians? What if everything fit neatly together for Christians? What if every time we tripped, an angel grabbed us before we hit the ground? What if God overruled all of my bad relational, business, and spiritual decisions—and always gave us a happy ending? Do you suppose that maybe people would come to Christ for all the wrong reasons?

Second, God knows how we humans tick. Enough is never enough. No matter how nice our car, our clothes, or our home, we always want more. So, would it follow that, even if God came and sat down with you personally, in a few weeks would you not begin to doubt the encounter, and start asking God to re-prove himself to you?

Third, throughout Scripture, God puts a high premium on faith. I don't know why—but he does. That's why our attempts to prove his existence, as good and helpful as they may be, all eventually come up short. At the end of every apologist's last argument, no matter how compelling it is, there still remains room for doubt among those who choose to cling to skepticism.

So I end where I began. These things I do know: God is real. He is there. And he cares. The rest of my questions will simply have to wait until I stand before him. Frankly, I can't wait. I'm glad I don't have enough faith *not* to believe in God.

40

SPEAK ONLY WHEN PEOPLE ARE READY TO LISTEN

It must have been amazing to have grown up as one of Jesus' brothers or sisters? I suppose that those half-siblings led an intriguing, confusing, exhilarating, and, sometimes, frustrating life. That's why I've always been a fan of Jesus' half brother, James. By the time he finally got around to writing the book in the Bible that bears his name, I suspect that James had seen it all. Maybe that's why the book of James is arguably the most brass tack, "just the facts ma'am," "get-her-done" book in the New Testament. This little self-help book gets to the heart of humanity with some of the most practical, down-to-earth advice I'm aware of anywhere. So when James warns about the misuse of the tongue, I listen. In short, he tells us that the tongue is a reckless appendage that is very hard to control or tame.

Some two thousand years after James wrote his essay on practical living, the Diggs household of the 1960s was learning its truth firsthand. Kindly put, I was not the easiest child to raise. My folks earned (but unfortunately never received) hazardous duty pay. One of my problems was an unruly tongue. I can still remember one day at the dinner table when Dad looked at me, totally exasperated, and said, "Steve, you know what they say about counting to ten before you speak? In your case, make it a hundred!"

I'm still fighting that battle—but thanks to dedicated parents, a better understanding of God's will, and a wife who doesn't hesitate to get in my face when I need it—today I'm doing better.

I was prompted to write this chapter after speaking at a West Texas church this past weekend. In one of my presentations I spoke on grace. And I made the case that we are saved by grace alone. After decades of trying to earn my way to God, I have come a point in life where I now believe that Romans 11:5 and Ephesians 2:8-9 cannot be ignored. In the latter passage, Paul restates the fact (five times) that we are saved by grace. Why? I think it was because he knew that humans have a hard time "hearing" that message. We want to believe that we can do something to *earn* our salvation.

Of course, to believe in grace doesn't mean that I believe God expects me to do nothing. Without repentance, acknowledging Jesus to be Lord, and a willingness to accept him in baptism we cannot receive his forgiveness. But salvation is a free gift from God. Sure, we must accept the free gift that God offers.

After my talk to the congregation, one of the church leaders took issue with me. He was still at a point in his life where he simply could not accept the notion that his works didn't help to save him. His argument was that he was afraid "some people" would misunderstand and not be willing to work for God if they accepted what I had said about grace.

At that moment, I had to make a decision. Should I debate this man and bluntly tell him how wrong I thought he was? Or should I ignore the comment and go on? Well, actually, I did something in between. I split the difference. For a few moments, we politely discussed our varying views, then we went onto another topic—both of us tacitly agreeing to disagree.

I use this to illustrate the fact that we are often presented with temptations to speak when silence might be the better option. Sure, the topic may be important. Sure, my human side wants to win an argument and pin the other guy to the floor. But is it best (or even right) to do so? Sometimes the best thing to do is zip it!

But when do I speak up? And when should I shut up?

Having spent much of my life doing this the wrong way, I determined several years ago to get serious about some self improvement. Let me share some things that I am learning.

1. Be sure that *you* are correct before you dare suggest that some-one else is wrong. Far too much of what masquerades as truth, fact, and established dogma is little more than personal prefer-ence and prejudice fueled by pride. This is where prayer, Bible study, and meditation come into play. These disciplines should be our first line of defense—not the last thing we do as we at-tempt to proof-text our argument.

2. Speak only to people who are ready to listen. You know what they say about casting pearls before swine. All the facts in the world mean nothing if the other person isn't ready to "hear" with her heart. Often that other person is so wrapped up in her own bagful of dysfunctional junk that she actually cannot hear a voice of reason.

   I'll never forget a ministry staff meeting that I attended several years ago. A heated debate broke out between two of the ministers. For me, the issue was crystal clear. I agreed with one minister and thought the other minister was obviously wrong. Finally, out of frustration, the first minister said, "What if I showed this to you in the Bible—then would you agree?"

   To which the other minister snapped, "No!"

   What do you do with that? All I know is to stop talking, find another topic, and give it time.

3. Never speak out of anger or a sense of superiority. When I really did a check-up on Steve Diggs, I realized that many of the disputes I became embroiled in were much more about me getting my way (or winning an argument) than they were

about getting to truth and exhibiting a gut-level love for the other person. Notches are for gunslingers—not friends with differing viewpoints.

4. Finally, pick your battles very carefully. Only make a stand when it is biblically mandated. In truth, most things are not worth debating. The Bible leaves a lot of things unsaid. Principles are prevalent, but specifics are seldom. While I would never suggest compromising on any command in Scripture, I would urge lots of flexibility with our feelings. For instance, in an earlier chapter I mention a church leader who proudly announced to me that, "We don't allow hand clapping around here." Frankly, I don't know for sure what he meant. Did he mean that they didn't allow clapping during the singing? Or applause at a baptism? Or joyful clapping to celebrate Jesus? But this I do know: the Bible is silent about clapping. Isn't such an edict from a church's leadership dangerous? What if the leadership's intolerance disheartened and ran weaker Christians away? What about the scriptures that warn against quenching the Spirit?

Contrast this to how another group of shepherds handled a similar problem. If my memory serves, it happened this way. When the kids became more expressive and began handclapping during church, some of the older folks didn't like it. Instead of maturely appreciating the youngsters' zeal for Jesus, they complained. So after discussing it, one of the shepherds stood before the church and announced, "We talked it over, and we've decided that from now on, if hand clapping offends you, you don't have to do it!" That was the end of that.

Life is too short to waste it telling others what to do when we should be listening for God's voice in our own hearts. Sometimes Steve just needs to zip it!

41

FOCUS ON THE
BIG PICTURE
WHEN GIVING

Many Christians struggle when someone approaches them to ask for money. I do. Over the decades I've gone from one extreme to another. There have been times when I felt guilty because I had more than the other person—so I gave. There have been times when I've been harsh and judgmental—so I didn't give. For many of us the question is, "Where is the balance in this?"

At many churches it is a weekly occurrence to receive phone calls from people who want "help" paying their utilities, making a car payment, buying gas, and on and on. Some of these calls are legitimate needs from people who have done their best and simply been decimated by real life. These are people who deserve, and should receive, our help. But far too many of these requests for help come from people who should be helping themselves. The dilemma is in knowing who is who.

For many Christians there is a tendency to piously think, "Oh well, I'm just going to give as often as I'm asked."

But maybe this is not piety. Could this be spiritual cowardliness, instead? There is a biblical concept called "stewardship." In a nutshell, good stewardship means realizing that God owns everything, and that he expects us do the best (and the most) with whatever he loans us. One day, the Master is going to call for an accounting of how we've used his stuff. To the point of this life chapter: God never asks his people to use his property to enable people for failure.

Now, is all of this a prelude to me railing against charitable causes? Nope. Am I opposed to helping the needy? Not at all. But I do want to challenge us to do a better job at determining *who* is truly needy, and *what* their real needs are.

If you have ever done any Third World travel, you realize that much of what masquerades as poverty in America, isn't. It seems that today's America has so watered down the definition of poverty that a family can own two cars and a plasma TV and still be getting a government check. Folks, something is wrong with this picture! This has fostered generations of people who have lost the capacity for proper shame. The current culture has more excuses than it has expectations for personal responsibility. I believe that Christians actually can do a disservice when we aide and enable such behavior. The net result of this is to encourage people who are doing wrong to continue doing wrong.

There was a time when charity was the last thing people would ask for. They worked longer hours, cut back to the bone, and moved in with family before they asked others to help. Rather than allowing the culture to redefine "need and poverty," Christians should search for God's heart on this matter. Paul told the early Christians, "For even when we were with you, we used to give you this order: if anyone is not willing to work, then he is not to eat, either" (2 Thessalonians 3:10, NASV).

The world that Jesus lived in was a most unforgiving place. It was filled with pain and suffering. Homeless people were starving and dying on the streets. We read lots of stories about Jesus' healings, but remember he didn't heal everyone who was sick or blind. He didn't feed everyone who had missed a meal. Jesus didn't come into the world to be a "fixer." Instead, Jesus maintained his mission—he kept his eye on the big picture. Most, if not all, of Jesus' miracles were aimed at helping people see that big picture. He helped people physically so they would realize his goodness and "Godness" and accept his teaching. Let's look at this familiar story together:

> During those days another large crowd gathered. Since they had nothing to eat, Jesus called his disciples to him and said, "I have compassion for these people; they have already been with me three days and have nothing to eat. If I send them home hungry, they will collapse on the way, because some of them have come a long distance." His disciples answered, 'But where in this remote place can anyone get enough bread to feed them?'
>
> "How many loaves do you have?" Jesus asked.
>
> "Seven," they replied.
>
> He told the crowd to sit down on the ground . . . he gave thanks for them also and told the disciples to distribute them. The people ate and were satisfied . . . About four thousand men were present. And having sent them away, he got into the boat . . . . (Mark 8:1-9, portions, NIV)

Let's notice some important things about this picnic on the grounds that Jesus hosted:

1. It was, if fact, driven by Jesus' compassion. But his compassion was directed at people who had apparently left homes and jobs for three days to learn more about God.
2. There was *true* need. The people in this story had gone without food for three days! They were hungry. And Jesus knew they would likely die trying to go all the way back home without a meal. This is far different from making a fifth car payment, or paying a cell phone bill, or buying pet food for someone who is too lazy to get, and keep, a job.
3. Jesus did not continue to feed them. He didn't set up a restaurant in the desert. No, he "sent them away." Jesus realized

the human need to be productive and do what we can for ourselves.

4. Jesus had his eye on the big picture. It is clear that part of
   Christ's purpose here was to build faith in his apostles. It
   wouldn't be long until they would see him crucified, and persecution would start. It was vital that they knew just how mighty
   God's power is.

Now for a word of balance as we close: Nothing here should be construed
as a license for selfishness or stinginess. Jesus is the one who tells us that we
represent him best when we give a cold glass of water, or clothe someone, or
visit a person in jail—in his name. My point is simply that throwing cash at
hurting people is often a bad substitute for what they may really need—a relationship with Jesus that goes beyond the temporal into the eternal. Sometimes
it's tough to remember the beautiful bye-and-bye when we're confronted
with the nasty now-and-now. Just remember: How we help, when we help,
and who we help, should all be driven by this long-term, big picture focusing
on the eternal.

42

PICK UP PENNIES

Fifty years ago a penny was actually worth something. In those days you could buy a piece of candy, pay the sales tax on a model airplane, or get your weight—all for a penny. These days it's a bit different. I understand that today a penny cost more to make than it's worth. Excluding the occasional creative (if not devious) sort, most of us don't really know what to do with a penny anymore. (I do recall the story of one fellow whose mail order business advertised a "copper etching of President Abraham Lincoln." His buyers sent large checks and got single pennies in return.) But despite its failure as a monetary motivator, my dad taught me an invaluable lesson with a penny.

Dad was a man of his times. In the 1950s and 60s most men made their mark by supporting their families and spending time teaching their kids important life lessons. My father was no exception. When I was a boy I remember that Dad never passed a penny on the ground without stopping to pick it up. As the years passed, and pennies became less valuable, this practice of his seemed more and more ridiculous to me.

Funny thing—that was over forty years ago and today I still pick up pennies. I realize that I'll never get rich doing this. (To earn eighteen dollars an hour I'd have to bend over 1800 times per hour; that'd be a penny pick up every two seconds. Not a good long-term investment plan.)

But there is an important life-skill in this that will serve you well: When we appreciate the small things in our lives, God tends to give us greater blessings.

This is evident in many people's lives who have made giving a top priority. I still remember a dear Christian brother who was wealthy. He could have bought and sold me twice in a day's time with the change that fell through the holes in his pockets. He used to explain his wealth by saying, "No matter how much I give—God out-gives me. It's as though he always has the bigger shovel." I believe one of the best ways to stay healthy is to stay busy doing good. Many people have found that one of the best ways to ward off depression is to become diligent in service to others. Paul reminded the early church, "You're far happier giving than getting." The fact is: The more we give to others, the more God seems to give to us.

You may have experienced this truth in your own life. Think about it. If you are a parent, don't you tend to pass more gifts to those kids who appreciate what they already have the most? If you are an employer, don't you prefer giving bonuses to those employees who thanked you profusely last year?

I wonder if this is one of the points that Jesus is communicating in his parable about the master who left town and entrusted his money to three different servants. As you probably will recall, he left one servant holding five talents, one with two, and one with only one talent. According to the Bible, the master determined who got what based on their abilities. So there was no honor or dishonor in who got the most or the least. Why? Because none of the servants had any control over the amount of ability (intelligence, wittiness, strength, etc.) with which God had equipped him. What each servant was held accountable for was the way he invested (appreciated) the gift he'd been given. When the master returned, he was thrilled to find the five and two talent servants had doubled their respective accounts. But the one talent guy had blown it. Excuses aside, he simply had not appreciated his master's gift enough to make the most of it that he could. And the master was ticked-off!

His master replied, "You wicked, lazy servant! . . . Take the talent from him and give it to the one who has the ten talents. For everyone who has will be given more, and he will have an abundance.

Whoever does not have, even what he has will be taken from him. And throw that worthless servant outside, into the darkness, where there will be weeping and gnashing of teeth." (portions of Matthew 25:26-30, NIV)

One the most despicable of all sins is ingratitude. When your gift is spurned by another, it hurts. When someone disrespects your efforts to show them honor, it angers you. When someone blows your kindness off without as much as a "Thank you," you're in no hurry to do anything else for that person.

Call it what you will. The "Appreciation Factor." The "too blessed to be stressed" view of life. Or the "attitude of gratitude." Dad never picked up pennies to get rich. He picked them up because he was grateful and appreciative, and felt that wastefulness was a sin. I am convinced that gratitude is one of the quickest ways to God's heart.

43

BE ALERT TO YOUR OWN IMPERFECTIONS

I believe in grace. Given the option, I would much prefer to err on the side of grace than towards that of works. But an important key to getting your life right is to understand that there is such a thing as righteous guilt. I know that that sounds like an oxymoron, but allow me to define what I mean. Righteous guilt is the guilt we have "earned" by our own bad behavior and, when admitted and accepted, leads to repentance and a desire for forgiveness.

If you don't get this big picture point, the standards for determining what is right and wrong will gradually erode in your life. Ye in our postmodern culture, making this distinction between right and wrong has become more critical and more difficult than ever before. You see, postmodernists (most of those in their mid-forties and younger) have been desensitized to this concept. Postmodernism rejects the notion that there are clear rights and wrongs. For this group, truth is relative. Their belief: "Whatever 'works' for me is right for me—but not necessarily right for the next person."

For those of us from the previous generation (we are known as "modernists"), this sounds like nonsense. We protest, "Rubbish! Truth is absolute. Some things *are* black and white—and to argue this fact is nonsensical!"

But how do we effectively debate such a proposition? It's as though someone has stepped up and said, "How long is a football field? True or False?"

139

"That," you respond, "is not a 'true or false' question! You make no sense."

Maybe part of the solution lies in the need for the modernists (we who are older and more rigid) to force ourselves over the fence. Maybe we need to look at things from the perspective of our postmodern friends. You see, from their perspective we are cold, unbending, and uncaring. They sometimes wonder out loud, "Where is the mystery of your faith? Where do you leave room for God to work in your life and speak to your heart?"

And to the degree that a modernist finds those questions uncomfortable, he makes the case for the postmodernist. We modernists have our own comfort zone—and most of us don't want anyone else messing with that zone or questioning our "established truths." After all, for centuries modernists have believed that if one simply stacks up enough facts, there will be an inevitable conclusion. To a postmodernist this sounds like the modernist is trying to put God in a box. A postmodernist sees this as our attempt to limit God.

What if we all admitted the truth? There is good and bad in both the modern and postmodern positions. This would mean that a modernist would have to admit that, far too often, he has tried to make all the pieces of God "fit" into his religious box. It would include the admission that God is big, and there is no way a finite brain can capture the wholeness of God. Further, it would include the painful admission that, while truth is not relative, no one person has fully captured all of God's truths. God is too deep, too rich, too powerful, and too wonderful for any one of us to fully possess or imagine. Despite our most gallant attempts to be perfect people, we all come up short, desperately needing the warmth of Jesus' arms. And while truth is universal, it is also true that God touches and deals with each of us in a most personal way.

Then, maybe our postmodern friends would begin to *hear* the fact that facts matter. Maybe we could come to the consensus that God speaks his truth in the Scriptures and those very Scriptures make a clear distinction between what is right and what is wrong. And truth must be universally applicable— unchanging. This would make Scripture our common and final arbitrator. Denying absolute right and wrong doesn't square with the nature of God.

It becomes what Dietrich Bonheoffer called "cheap grace." Anything that Jesus died for isn't cheap. Grace is free—but it isn't cheap. When we receive God's graceful forgiveness, it will provoke in us the desire to do right. How do I know this? It's what Jesus said: "If anyone wishes to come after me, he must deny himself, and take up his cross and follow me. For whoever wishes to save his life will lose it; but whoever loses his life for my sake will find it" (Matthew 16: 24-25, NIV).

To follow God means that we acknowledge the truth Paul wrote to the Romans, "For all have sinned and fall short of the glory of God" (8:23). Simply put, righteous guilt leads us to admit that we are wrong and drives us with a dogged determination to be right.

44

BE READY TO SPEAK

Last night was quite a night. We met a special person. Forgive me for being cloak-and-daggerish here, but instead of me giving you his name, for the purposes of this life chapter, I'll simply call him Jim. (Later you will understand why he deserves anonymity.) Most importantly, last night God was at work. Fortunately, for once, I had my spiritual antenna up when God nudged. Before I tell you more about last night, let me give you a little back story so this will all make sense.

Since Bonnie was a teen, Jim has been one of her favorite singers. In the 1960s and the 1970s his Emmy Award-winning weekly variety show was a staple for families nationwide. Over the decades he has had countless hit records—including more than twenty gold and platinum albums. He still performs to enthusiastic audiences around the globe. So when we had an opportunity a week ago to get tickets to his show, it was a no brainer. Last night we went to hear him sing his hits.

Yesterday, earlier in the day, there had been some talk about Bonnie and me being invited backstage after the concert to meet Jim personally. We were excited—and probably a bit too expectant. When we got to the venue, the theater manager told me that Jim was rushing to leave town in the morning and might not have time to visit with us after the show. Then, just before curtain time, he came down to our seats and kindly explained that, in fact, Jim would not be able to socialize after the performance. We were both disappointed, but hey, we had seats on the third row—we were just excited to be able to see the show!

Sitting next to me was a nice fellow who identified himself as a personal friend of Jim's. We spoke to one another several times during the show. Near the end of the concert, my new buddy leaned over and said, "Jim is leaving town tomorrow to go to the bedside of his best friend who is dying." Suddenly it all made sense. My personal disappointment was replaced with sadness for Jim. And Jim's performance immediately made more sense to me. Although still the consummate professional, I'd detected a bit less heart and bravado than I had expected from Jim's performance. As he was singing his final numbers, I hurt for Jim. In my heart I prayed, "God, I don't know if Jim is a Christian or not, but if I can hold Jesus up and minister to him—make it happen." Even as I ended the prayer, I thought to myself, "What are the odds?"

A few minutes later, as the show closed and the house lights came up, I noticed the theater manager motioning to us. When we stepped over to him he said quietly, "Jim has changed his mind and has asked to meet with you. He's never changed his mind like this before. Follow me." In a blur, Bon and I were being ushered through the crowd and past a security door. Walking quickly through the back of the stage, the manager stopped as we arrived at a door with Jim's name on it. A knock at the door—and we were inside. The office was opulent and beautiful—filled with fabulous art, a grand piano which was covered with dozens of photographs, and at least one of Jim's Emmy Awards.

I realized that this was more than a mere meet and greet. I was still curious as to why Jim had changed his mind about inviting us back. After a few moments of pleasantries, Jim told me he had been reading from one of my books. Wow, isn't it amazing how God controls the events of our lives? God had taken me up on my offer to minister to Jim! I realized that we were there on a mission. I searched for the courage to do what I knew I must. Finally, I stammered, "Jim, we don't know one another, but I have the sense that you are in some real pain at the moment."

He could have rightfully demanded, "What gives you that idea?" Or, "How dare you delve into my private life!" But instead, he gently admitted, "You're right. My best friend, Pierre, is dying and I'm leaving the country tomorrow to be with him."

I collected enough words to say, "Jim, I certainly don't want to be presumptive, but would you allow us to pray with you in this difficult moment?"

I wasn't sure what to expect (nor was the theater manager who, by now, was standing there with his mouth wide open), but Jim said, "Yes, please do."

So we held hands and I prayed to God, in Jesus' name, that he would bless this tough time in Pierre and Jim's lives and that he would be their strength. Frankly, I don't remember what else I said in the prayer.

Now, if you're expecting me to relate some miraculous, spur-of-the-moment conversion experience, I have to disappoint you. It didn't happen that way.

But here is what happened. God's name was honored and his power over the present and the future was acknowledged. A seed was planted. Hopefully, as I write this, Jim is pondering our moment with God on his plane trip.

So much of what we Christians can do to share Jesus comes in the smallest ways and at the least expected moments. The key is always to be ready to pick up and travel light for God. Last night was not the time to pull out my Bible and start preaching. It was a special moment in time when God allowed us to establish a beachhead for him. Jesus said it this way, "Let your light so shine before man that they may see your Father . . . ."

I figure that any God who is strong enough to change a performer's heart in the middle of his show and ask me back to see him, is strong enough to put other people in that same singer's path who will light the road to God a bit further.

Your job and my job is really quite simple: Be ready to speak a word in Jesus' name. We don't have to be overly overt or intrusive—Jesus never was. We should never embarrass another person. Last night I was tentative in the way I asked Jim if we could pray. I made it easy for him to decline my offer. And if he had, it wouldn't have been me that he was rejecting.

No matter where, or how far, God takes you in this world remember that you are his ambassador. There is a bigger picture than our human eyes can see or our minds can comprehend.

Watch for "coincidences" from God. Don't ignore the "chance meetings" that he allows. Actually, it all goes back to that phrase we learned in that childhood song, about letting our Christian lights shine. We are his lights in this world. Wherever we go, we simply need to keep our lights with us.

So I ask, "Hey buddy, have you got a light?"

45

DETERMINE WHAT KIND OF RUNNER YOU ARE

This is the life chapter where I want to challenge you to decide: Are you a sprinter or a marathon runner? You are probably one or the other. This doesn't necessarily mean you can't do both. It just means you are not best at both.

Before I go further, let's define our terms. I'm speaking metaphorically. This is not the sort of running where we'll discuss which type of running shoes we prefer, New Balance or Nikes. And you won't work up a sweat—at least not physically. Instead, I'm asking a much more profound and probing question. This is the moment before the mirror when you honestly ask yourself for an answer that you probably already know in your soul. This is when you speak truth to yourself and admit that you are either a sprinter or a marathon runner. The wisdom of the ages acknowledges that different people have different talents and skill sets. Parents are taught to raise each child in "the way he should go." Why? Because each child is born with a "bent."

Real world parents understand that no two kids are the same. Children are born with different temperaments, talents, and abilities. From the day they're hatched, some kids are sprinters and others are marathon runners.

A sprinter is a person who does his best work in "short burst" situations. He blows in, blows up, and blows out. A sprinter tends to be kinetic and driven. This person is results oriented. He can easily annoy, alienate, and frustrate everyone in his world. He may not be the best guy to go fishing with—unless you're talking four hours of deep sea fishing in a high-powered boat. You probably don't want to lose a board game to a sprinter. He may not be the most touchy-feely guy at the party. And he is passionate—about everything.

However, in a pinch, a sprinter can be the best friend in the world. He's really good to have around on the day you fall over in the store with a heart attack. His "get 'er done" approach to things may save your life. He will rush to the pain reliever aisle and grab a box of aspirin to stick in your mouth. (And much to the chagrin of the marathon runner, he won't stop at the resister to pay for them!) He'll be sure that you get CPR while speed dialing 911. He'll kick down walls to get you to the hospital—and make sure that you're on the front burner at the emergency room. In a moment of crisis you will have no better friend than a sprinter. But, as you recover over the next several weeks, don't expect much help from the sprinter. In his mind the emergency is now past and he is on to other things.

In contrast, a marathon runner is the long-term, always-at-your-side, steady-as-she-goes person. Marathon runners take time to smell the roses. As a matter of fact, a marathon runner is likely to string up a hammock at the rose garden and s-l-o-w-l-y smell every rose—again and again and again!

As you recover from that heart attack, the marathon runner is also the one who will be at your side day and night. Marathon runners have stamina. They don't wilt, wither, or withdraw when times are tough and nights are long. Marathon runners will patiently listen, and re-listen, to the same old stories you told them *before* the Alzheimer's sat in. No matter how dreary, desperate, or depressed you are—your marathon buddy will be there to hold your hand. She rarely glances at her watch, and will never, ever run off with her hands over her ears screaming, "I wish I were a sprinter!"

Our unwillingness to get into the other runner's shoes is why marathon runners and sprinters sometimes don't get along. For instance, sprinters always want to "fix" things. This tendency can easily drive a marathon runner to distraction. Marathon runners frequently want to simply discuss a problem because the matriculation process is, in itself, therapeutic. But the sprinter doesn't "get it." The way he sees it: "Don't come to me with a problem if you don't want me to fix it. That's what we sprinters do. If all you want to do is talk and talk and talk about it—find another marathon runner!"

Following are three ideas that may help you be better at whichever of the two you are—and be more capable of dealing with others who are not like you.

1. Decide which you are—and celebrate it. Because anyone who succeeds in business must have some of both attributes, I have learned to do both. But by nature I'm a sprinter. This is both good and bad. Over the years I've come to a degree of peace in this knowledge. For many of my younger years I went from one extreme to the other: sometimes feeling guilty for being a sprinter, and at other times angry that I wasn't more appreciated for it. In more recent years, I've realized that this is the "bent" that I was born with. God must have designed and engineered me this way for a reason. I need to be thankful to him. In fact, this knowledge has helped me in ministry. I do my best work coming into a church for only a few hours or days. I help them strap on a jetpack for Jesus—then I'm gone. This isn't to say that I don't admire the marathon ministers who birth, baptize, and bury their folks. But that's just not my gift.

2. Don't criticize the other type of runner. Sprinters and marathon runners often don't get along. They each tend to see the other's differences as character flaws instead of precisely what makes them beautiful and totally essential. Sprinters marvel at how slow marathon runners run—sometimes wondering

if they actually still have a pulse. Conversely, marathon runners wonder if sprinters are anything more than living heart
donors. While there are good and appropriate moments to
discuss God's will for the other person's life, often it's best to
allow God to do most of the convicting. Whether we realize
it or not, sprinters and marathon runners have a symbiotic
relationship. I believe God planned it this way. (I wonder if
this could be further evidence that God has a sense of humor.)
Remember, it was God who gave that runner his or her "bent."

3. Sand down your own rough edges. Rather than criticize others,
I need to busy myself conforming to God's will for my life.
Whether you're a sprinter or a marathon runner, you will tend
to get off course. Extremes are usually bad things. Don't allow
the bad side of your personal "bent" to define you. Constantly
reevaluate your deeds and your motives. Paul may have had the
Olympic Games of his day in mind when he said,

You've all been to the stadium and seen the athletes race. Everyone
runs; one wins. Run to win. All good athletes train hard. They do
it for a gold medal that tarnishes and fades. You're after one that's
gold eternally. I don't know about you, but I'm running hard for
the finish line. I'm giving it everything I've got. No sloppy living
for me! I'm staying alert and in top condition. I'm not going to
get caught napping, telling everyone else all about it and then
missing out myself. (1 Corinthians 9:24-27, The Message)

46

LAY DOWN
YOUR PRIDE

People react differently when imperfections in their lives are brought to light. How do you respond? Do you feel a warm tingle run down your spine? That warm feeling can be a good thing or a bad thing. If it's that horrible, painful feeling of having really made a mess of things, it might lead to improvement (a good thing.) But if the warmth you feel is your blood beginning to boil because someone has dared to confront and challenge your behavior, it is likely a bad thing.

At the core of much sin is pride. Pride is sort of the universal, one-size-fits-all sin. Most other faults come from pride. "But," you may say, "what does pride have to do with lust, or greed, or telling a lie?"

Doesn't most lust (the desire to have something that isn't rightfully yours) come from a prideful heart that believes it has a "right" to take what it wants? Isn't greed (the drive to acquire what we don't need or deserve) fueled by a prideful heart that believes the commercials on television that reassure us that "we're worth it?" And aren't many of our lies told to save face and pretend to be better than we are?

David was a king who fell to his pride, but refused to be beaten by it. His theft of another man's wife was born of arrogance and a sense of kingly entitlement. Then his pride (fear of being caught) led him to exasperate the situation by murdering the woman's husband. But after the deed was done, David set aside his pride long enough to hear the voice of God speaking through a friend. Nathan came to David with a parable about two men. One was a wealthy rancher who owned herds of sheep. The other was a poor man with a single lamb that was his pet. When the wealthy man decided to have lamb chops for dinner, he stole and butchered his poor neighbor's single sheep. As David listened to the story, his blood began to boil as he roared, ".... the man who did this deserves to die! He must pay for that lamb four times over, because he did such a thing and had no pity" (2 Samuel 12: 5b-6, NIV).

With those words still tumbling from David's own mouth, Nathan looked at his friend and said, "You are the man." Can you imagine what must have rushed through David's head at that moment? He essentially had four options. The first three are what I call the dangerous "Ds."

- Deny. David could have denied that he had done such a thing. Haven't we all done this? There we stand—red-handed—claiming that we didn't commit the offense. Logically speaking, this is stupid behavior. But we still run it up the flagpole hoping that someone will believe it.
- Deflect. David might have deflected the guilt by claiming that the woman had tempted him, or that her husband deserved what he got, or that some kingdom flunky had pimped the woman to him. Some of us have become very effective with this little technique. But by blaming others (who, in fact, may be partly to blame), I miss the big picture: It's my own, personal sin we are discussing.
- Disengage. Another popular way that rich and powerful people get out of tight spots is to simply disengage. Power has its privileges. People with clout, like David, can stop an unpleasant conversation by ending a meeting and excusing their underlings. If that falls short, a person with power can always fire, disinherit,

divorce, or otherwise push anyone who is courageous enough to stand his ground.

There was a fourth option. David could do the right thing. Thankfully, that is the option that the king selected. Instead of denying, deflecting, or disengaging, David admitted, acknowledged, and accepted his guilt with the simple statement, "I have sinned against the Lord." He laid down his pride. In that single, grief-stricken moment God forgave David and wrapped his arms around him. There were, to be sure, punishments and consequences. Remember, forgiveness from God doesn't necessarily mean that the pain is over. David's sin brought shame to the kingdom and death to his baby son. But David's humility allowed him to remain a "man after God's own heart."

So which will you do when you've done wrong and someone has brought it to your attention: deny, deflect, disengage, or repent?

47

CHERISH THE INTERRUPTIONS

86,400. That's the number of seconds in one day. If you are like me, those are pretty full seconds. Most days I feel as if I'm on one of those Japanese bullet trains—flying past people and opportunities. Everything is a blur as I blow through the day at a 100 mph. Frequently, I'm barely able to get the urgent things done. And sadly, far too often, the important matters are simply left undone.

One of the things that bugs me the most (I'm not proud to confess this) is that sometimes I become angry at people and events that interrupt my schedule. Whether it's an email from Bonnie asking me to run an unexpected errand; or someone with a broken car who obviously needs my help; or one of the kids who wants to re-talk something that we've already discussed nineteen times—I am frequently disappointed by my lack of patience.

I still don't have this demon conquered, but over the years God has helped me face this problem—and make some headway.

The single most important turning point for me came one day when I approached Dr. Jerry Jones, one of my mentors, to discuss an issue I was dealing with. Jerry is one of the busiest, highest octane guys I know. He travels, writes, speaks, and teaches nationwide. Thousands of people seek his counsel on spiritual and marital issues. He is constantly being pulled by one person, then the next, for his time and attention. So I began my conversation slowly

153

and hesitantly by saying, "Jerry, I hate to pester you because I know you're extremely busy . . . ."

That was the last word out of my mouth before I saw his face turn from friendly to almost angry. Jerry looked me squarely in the eye and said, "Steve, don't *ever* say a thing like that to me again! I am never too busy to spend time with you."

Whew! Was I supposed to feel better—or scared?

Jerry went on, "My job is to be like our Lord. Jesus ran a ministry of interruptions. He frequently started to do one thing only to be interrupted by someone who needed his time more immediately."

Frankly, I don't even remember what I wanted to discuss with Jerry on that particular day. But in the years since, I've played and re-played Jerry's words in my mind a number of times: "Jesus ran a ministry of interruptions."

The more I've pondered it, the more truth I saw in it. Over the years since that day it has occurred to me how often Jesus began doing one thing only to be interrupted and end up doing something else. Jesus always seemed to live in the moment. Over and over, his plans were preempted. Do you remember the day that he got an urgent message from an important religious leader asking him to come and heal his dying daughter? Immediately Jesus began to follow Jairus to his home. No doubt this was a high-profile event. Likely there were thousands of people following. This was Jesus' chance to heal an important Jewish leader's child and become more popular than ever in the better social circles. If Jesus had had a publicist, he would have advised, "Stay on task Jesus—keep moving. You want everyone to see you perform this miracle." But things didn't work out as planned. On his way to Jairus' house, a common woman with an uncontrolled hemorrhage reached out for healing. Jesus could simply have ignored her and rushed on. But that wasn't the Jesus style. Instead, he stopped and spent time becoming acquainted with this otherwise unremarkable woman.

This was not the exception in Jesus' life—it was the norm. Even when things were at their worst, Jesus still kept his periscope up—always ready to respond to the immediate needs around him. I don't operate that way. The more stressful my situation becomes, the less likely I am to pay attention to others who need my help. I want to be more like Jesus.

Luke tells how Jesus started to Jerusalem fully aware that, when he arrived, his enemies would murder him on a cross. To prepare his followers, Jesus said, "We are going up to Jerusalem, and everything that is written by the prophets about the Son of Man will be fulfilled. He will be handed over to the Gentiles. They will mock him, insult him, spit on him, flog him and kill him" (18:31-32, NIV).

Now if this had been me, I would have been so focused on my own problems that I wouldn't have noticed anyone else's pain. But not Jesus. On his own death march, Jesus stopped and healed a blind beggar. Then, a few miles down the road, he stopped long enough to change the life of a short, corrupt tax collector named Zaccheus. This little guy had spent his career enriching himself by ripping off his fellow Jews. But thanks to Jesus' willingness to be interrupted, Zaccheus found hope, forgiveness, and morphed from a taker into a giver.

Even when Jesus was moments from his own arrest, he still took time to heal the ear of one of his captors who would aid and abet his crucifixion.

We humans tend to miss the big picture in two ways. One, when we mistakenly think that what is most important to us is also what is most important to God. And two, when we adopt the attitude that says "it's my time." Remember, as Christians we have given it all up for God. Whether it's our money or our music, our talents or our toasters—it's all God's stuff. The basic concept of biblical stewardship means realizing that God owns everything, including our time. Remembering this is why Jesus never missed the big picture.

The point here is simple: If you and I want to have true peace and joy, we must pattern our lives after the one who brings peace and joy. I know that this is counterintuitive stuff. This is not the way most of our friends think. According to the media, we get ahead by putting ourselves first. Most awards are given to self-promoters. But in God's economy (the only one that will survive into eternity), it has much more to do with how available and ready we are when God "interrupts" our day.

48

DECIDE WHICH IS MOST IMPORTANT: WHO YOU KNOW OR WHAT YOU KNOW

This life chapter can be easily misunderstood, so give me a wide berth as I share this thought. Allow me to build the watch before I give you the time.

The Christian world that I grew up in believed that Christianity was more about *what* we knew than *who* we knew. I grew up thinking that if I could just learn enough about God, he would be happy with me. I don't believe that anymore. Today, I believe more than ever before that being Christian is a blend of both *who* and *what* we know. I'm disturbed by the dearth of Bible knowledge in today's church. But it hasn't always been that way. I can remember a story that goes back two or three generations. In those days when a court didn't have a Bible to swear on, I'm told that they would invite a Christian to come up, put their hands on him (instead of a Bible)—because Christians were known to know the Scriptures. In my own childhood there was still a high premium put on Bible study. I can still remember the daily devotionals in our home. And I remember the way Mom forced me to sit down on Saturday afternoons and fill out all the Scripture quotes in my Sunday school lesson book. Not so today.

God's kids (including this one) don't study the Word the way we should. I have the sense that one day in heaven many of us will be very sorry that we didn't spend more time in this earthly realm getting to know our God and his Word. Giving instruction to his protégé Timothy, Paul encouraged the young man to "study to show yourself approved unto God . . . rightly dividing the word of truth" (paraphrased from 2 Timothy 2:15,KJV).

If you are not in the Word on a regular basis, you should be. I'm aware that some Christians are convinced that there is a "right" way to study the Bible. Some suggest reading the entire Bible every year. Others encourage deep, long-term study of smaller portions. Many people believe that the best time to study their Bible is early in the morning. For others getting up early is like being persecuted for righteousness sake. Often these people find that reading just before bed, or late in the afternoon while on the Stair Master, is more effective. I won't give you any formulas here, because I haven't found any one-size-fits-all approach that works. Since God made each of us differently, maybe it's best not to try to shoe-horn another Christian into your preferred approach. The point is: God's people should be students of God's Word.

But let me share something that I didn't used to believe: I'm not convinced that Bible study (*what* we know) is as important as *who* we know. The facts are these: Knowing God is much easier when we study our Bibles; but it is possible to be a Bible scholar and still never really get to know the *who* of the Bible.

Remember, in the first century the Bible (at least what we call the New Testament) didn't exist. And while there were a few copies of the Old Testament available in synagogues and an occasional letter from one of the Apostles, there was very little access to Scripture for the typical early Christian—who was also probably illiterate. So why did the church enjoy explosive growth? What did these people learn that turned them from the rankest forms of paganism to a life of self-control, morality, and holiness? What happened that made many of them willing to endure persecution, loss of jobs, and, in some cases, execution?

I believe that these first generation Christians put their primary emphasis on *Who* they knew. This led to the heart, the passion, and the fire-in-the-gut that made Christianity a lifestyle rather than a one-hour Sunday morning event when they looked at the back of the head in the pew in front—and then went home.

Knowing *about* God is good (and vital) but it isn't the same as *knowing* God. Jesus had an amazingly simple way of presenting his viewpoint: Love God with everything you have, and learn to love others as you already love yourself. Granted, this doesn't speak directly to the need for repentance, confession, baptism, holy living, and a host of other doctrinal matters. But if we simply look at God the way Jesus looked at God, the rest of these matters will dovetail together. It's a matter of seeing the big picture.

49

LEAD WITH
YOUR HEART

One of the most dangerous things a Christian can do is fail to understand how God built us. Granted, God engineered and designed us to operate on various levels. Misunderstanding this point causes a lot of religious confusion. God's directives to his children sometimes seem contradictory. For instance, Jesus clearly manifested love for his parents. But, at one point, he also told his followers that they must hate their parents in order to be his disciples. So which is it? Are we supposed to love or hate our parents? Despite what some skeptics have suggested, Jesus was not contradicting himself. Any fair minded person who elects to read these different passages within their rightful context will see this.

In a similar way, it is accurate to say that God expects us to have both an intellectual faith and an experiential faith. We need both dimensions of faith to sustain us through the roughest, loneliest, and most despondent seasons of life. I believe that nothing can take the place of a well thought out, clearly articulated, and thoroughly researched faith. I believe, with Peter, that Christians should "always be prepared to give an answer to everyone who asks . . . for the hope that you have" (1 Peter 3:15, NIV). Much of our relationship with God is built on what we learn from sources such as the Bible, teachers, and mentors. But a great part of our walk should be built on what we have personally seen, touched, and witnessed as God has worked in our lives.

This is what I call leading with our hearts. You see, God built you from the DNA out to be a person of the heart. But this is a concept that far too few Christians ever comprehend. Sadly, the outside world seems to understand this better than many Christians. Think about it. Have you ever seen a McDonalds' television commercial that "spoke" to your head? I'll bet you've never seen an ad where some guy, wearing a white lab jacket, stood in front of the camera and said, "Hi, I'm from McDonalds and we sell hamburgers. They taste great—never mind the fact that if you eat too many you may need a triple bypass. Plus we make a good profit selling them to you. Thank you very much."

Have you ever seen that commercial? Nope. And you're not going to because McDonalds knows that that isn't the way to sell hamburgers.

Instead, McDonalds speaks to our hearts. I didn't notice a McDonalds TV commercial last Christmas, but one might go like this: It would open in a living room with a beautiful, glowing fireplace. Next to the fireplace is a gorgeously decorated Christmas tree. And on the floor next to the tree is a little round table. Standing beside the little round table is Billy. Now Billy is about four years old and he's putting cookies on the table top. About that time, big brother comes dribbling his basketball through the living room. He stops and looks over his shoulder at Billy and demands, "What are you doing?"

Billy says, "Oh, I'm putting out cookies for Santa Claus. He's coming tonight, you know?"

"Billy," his brother retorts, "there's no such thing as Santa." And with that, he leaves behind a crushed, broken shell of a little brother. "No such thing as Santa?!?"

Next scene: It's the middle of the night and everyone in the house is sound asleep—except Billy. He's lying upstairs in his bed, holding his blanket and his teddy bear, and he's crying. "No Santa?" he ponders, "I know what I'll do! I'll go downstairs and check. If my cookies are gone—that proves that there's a Santa Claus!"

So Billy gets out of his bed and walks down the dark hall and down the steps into the living room. The room is dark, but the fireplace is still glowing.

When Billy reaches the Christmas tree his little feet glue to the floor. He gets his courage up and walks around to the other side of the tree to the little round table. Slowly, Billy turns his gaze down to the table . . . and his heart breaks as he sees that his cookies are still there. There's no Santa! Billy turns to go back to bed. But just as his foot hits the first step, a big, white gloved hand drops down on his little set of shoulders and the voice from the hand says, "Billy, I'm sorry I'm late—but I always love your cookies. Merry Christmas."

Then up comes the signature: "Merry Christmas from your friends at McDonalds."

Now let me ask you a simple question: Which one of those two commercials gets to where you live? The guy in the lab jacket—or Billy?

We are people of the heart. God built us that way. When we lead with our hearts, things change for the better—forever. Cold marriages warm up. Parent/child relationships warm up. Squabbles at church seem less important. And most importantly, others who don't know Jesus will be touched by our hearts far more than our words.

50

LET YOUR LOVE
DEMONSTRATE ITSELF

B e honest. When you go to a baseball game don't you dream of catching a foul ball? And wouldn't it really be cool if you caught it in mid-flight—and on television as the world watched and cheered? That's exactly what happened last night at the Phillies stadium when Steve Monforto (who's been going to Philly games since he was three) finally caught his first foul ball. It was the middle of the fifth inning when Washington player Jason Werth fouled a pop into the stands where Steve and his three-year-old daughter, Emily, were sitting. Steve sprung to his feet and made an amazing catch. The crowd cheered. But instead of holding his prize ball to his chest, he high-fived Emily and gently handed the ball he had waited a lifetime for to his young daughter. Without missing a beat, Emily promptly turned to the railing directly in front of her and fired her new ball away to fans on a lower tier!

In that split second, as the cameras continued shooting and the fans in the neighboring bleachers gasped, Steve's smiling face looked momentarily stunned. He must have thought, "Did she *really* do that! What's the deal—that was my prized ball and she threw it away!"

Also in that moment, as time seemed to stand still, Emily turned back around to look at her dad's face. Steve recounted on today's news that, in that instant, Emily realized her mistake by the stunned look on his face. Then, he told reporters, Emily's face registered regret as she realized that she'd disappointed her dad who was still wearing his backwards-turned Phillies cap.

As only a dad can do, Steve immediately realized the hurt and brokenness his child was feeling. The smile that had permeated his face only a moment earlier as he caught his ball returned as he looked into Emily's eyes. With a smile of fatherly love (that I can't find the words here to describe) Steve reached for Emily in a heartbeat and pulled her tightly to his chest—and hugged the uncertain three-year-old. Whether he still missed his ball or not, I can't tell you. But his face was a wall-to-wall smile, glowing with love for his little one.

As I recall, sports writer Mark Newman phrased it this way: "It was more than one of those many little moments in the course of a long baseball game .... This moment was truly Beyond Baseball. It was the real glory of the game right there in front of you, a father hugging his little girl to assure her . . . ."

This evening, as I have watched that video clip over and over, one thought keeps ringing in my brain: This was God in human skin. No, I'm not suggesting that Steve Monforto is anymore God than you or me. But what he did was Godlike.

Do you remember the story of the prodigal son? The story deals with a rich man who had two sons. One, the younger, insulted his father by demanding his inheritance early. His father gave it to him and the boy headed off the farm to seek fame and fortune and lots of babes. But things didn't work so well for him in the big city. Finally, with his money wasted and his morals compromised, he returned home humiliated. He'd already gotten in front of a mirror to practice what he'd say to his dad in the hopes that maybe he could get a job working on the farm. But the Bible makes some interesting observations that give us insight into his father (who, by the way, actually represents God himself). The Bible says, "But while he was still a long way off, his father saw him and was filled with compassion for him; he ran to his son, threw his arms around him and kissed him."

The Bible tells us that his father saw him returning from a long distance down the road. A fair question here would be to ask, how come? Why did Dad see his son so far off? Do you suppose that in his heart, he had never taken his eyes off his son? Maybe Dad's daily ritual was to stand by the window and search the horizon for his wandering son.

Also, did you notice that the father didn't wait for the son to come to him? Instead, this father ripped out the front door and ran headlong to get to his son. And when he arrived there was no chastisement or "I told you so's." Instead, like Steve Monforto, he threw his arms around the boy and kissed him. In a blink, everything was forgiven in a sea of forgetfulness.

I suspect that Monforto's "God behavior" will have long lasting impact.

- How many dads and moms do you suppose have been challenged to be better parents because they saw this remarkable video on television or YouTube?
- For the rest of her life little Emily will never forget how big and broad and inclusive her daddy's arms were. I suspect she will be a better parent as she reflects her dad's behavior towards her own kids. Lastly, this was a fresh sip of living water for an increasingly hostile and selfish culture. In other news today, there were three very different stories (one about a politician, one about an athlete, and one about a performer) who had each acted selfishly and rudely towards others. So here on a day when we most needed it, America was reminded of what I call the "God spark."

Thank you, Steve Monforto, for showing us the "God spark" by your behavior. In a very human way, you have reminded us all of the goodness of the real Father. Long before last night's Phillies game, Jesus was already describing what a good Father our God is, "Which of you fathers, if your son asks for a fish, will give him a snake instead? . . . If you then, though you are evil, know how to give good gifts to your children, how much more will your Father in heaven give the Holy Spirit to those who ask him!"

51

TAKE PERSONAL RESPONSIBILITY

M any people in our culture believe a dangerous lie. Today, we live in the *United States of Victimology*. It seems that a growing number of Americans have long ago abrogated personal responsibility in exchange for a mindset that panders to their own personal pity. Everywhere we look we see people who are intent on being victims.

This is the attitude that allows someone to spill hot coffee in his lap—and then blame his host. It's the viewpoint that leads a person to go into a Burger King and come out *looking* like a Whooper—and then blame the restaurant! And sure enough, we can usually find a lawyer on a billboard who is willing to help get some money out of the deal.

But what is missed here is that the difference between winners and losers is usually far less circumstantial than the loser wants to admit. A loser is a person who spends his life sitting in a pity puddle saying, "I've been ripped off, cheated, lied to, and kicked around—and I'm just going to sit here until someone fixes my problems."

A winner, on the other hand, is the person who says, "Yep! I've been ripped off, cheated, lied to, and kicked around. But you know what? I'm not going to allow other people to dictate the terms of my life. With the help of God, starting right here, right now, I'm going to draw a bead on the horizon to where I believe God wants me to go in this life. And then, one step at a time, I'm going to doggedly follow that heading!"

The victim identity panders to the worst and the basest within a person. It refocuses the blame for one's own failure onto others. And when we do that we disempower ourselves because we are effectively ceding the control of our lives to those other people. This is why many well-intentioned government programs—designed to help deserving people through a short, tough time—have grown into bureaucratic behemoths that drain our national resources. There was a time when respectable people hated the thought of accepting handouts. But gradually over the decades, handouts became acceptable and even expected. We called them charities. Charities became welfare programs. And today, the welfare programs are called entitlements. And when any group is constantly told that they are entitled to anything, it won't be long before they believe it. This kills appropriate human dignity, initiative, and incentive. When people aren't challenged to perform at peak levels, they rarely do. Potential is squandered and lives are wasted.

And as people feel less and less able to control their destiny, they become angry. They spend so much time and energy blaming others that they rarely see the good in the world all around them.

If you identify with this struggle, let me share three ideas that you might find helpful aids as you readjust your worldview.

1. Understand that God has already given you a very special skill set—and he intends for you to use it to his glory. One day, God will look you squarely in the eye and ask for an accounting. Peter Drucker says, "The best way to predict the future is to create it." Admittedly, God is in ultimate control of all that exists. But he allows each individual a great deal of flexibility and influence over his or her own destiny. God gave us brains, strength, and time. It is our responsibility to exhaust these talents as creatively, efficiently, and gloriously as

possible. Every Christian should be dedicated to wearing out before rusting out.

2. Strive for excellence at whatever you do. Learn to appreciate the true joy that fills the human heart when a challenge is met and a goal is achieved. Winners are the ones who get onto the gridiron of life. No one likes to be tackled, hit, or hurt. But oh, those touchdowns! They make every moment of pain and drudgery worth it. Granted, the guys sitting on the bench may never get their jerseys torn or their faces bloodied, but they will never know the sheer joy of exhausting their last ounce of strength to lay the football across the goal line either.

3. Learn to appreciate the opportunities you *are* given and don't complain over the ones you are not given. You can't control the gifts you receive. But you can control how you "redeem the time." How you develop your talents is up to you. Far too many of us waste the precious "three score and ten" (a biblical reference to the seventy years of life that many people are given) by simply watching from the stands. These are the people who never get to play—or even to sit on the bench and enjoy being part of the team. Instead, they spend their lives in the stands booing and jeering the ones who are playing the game.

Not to strain a metaphor too much, but let me share a quote attributed to Bear Bryant, the legendary Alabama football coach: "The trouble with the road to success is that it's lined with too many parking places."

Here are two key questions that we must grapple with if we hope to enjoy the ultimate "win." Am I allowing the "noise" of a negative world to camouflage God's plan for my life? Or am I aggressively searching for God's big picture for me, and then joyfully hugging it tightly in my arms and running for the goalpost as if my life depends on it?

52

HOLD TO PRINCIPLES THAT LAST

In many areas, what was considered wrong, even reprehensible, a few years ago, today is considered right and respectable. For instance, in the 1970s when I was a young broadcaster, no one would have dared use profanity on air. If a deejay slipped and said a "bad word," he immediately went back on mic to apologize—hoping that he wouldn't be fired. Today, it seems that there is more profanity and vulgarity on the airwaves (don't even get me started on cable) than there are commercials. To many of us, it seems that our culture is "slouching toward Gomorrah," as Judge Robert Bork put it.

In various other life chapters, I have pointed to positive solutions from the Scriptures to help us live holy, fulfilling lives. But in this visit I don't plan to go back thousands of years for our advice. Instead, let's go back about fifty or sixty years.

But I'm getting ahead of myself. First, a little background. Last week Bonnie and I had a few days off between commitments, so we decided to take a little vacation. We had waited too late to get frequent flyer-miles tickets to Europe, so we decided to make a car trip to a decidedly less high-brow destination. We loaded up and headed for Branson, Missouri. Yeah, yeah—I've heard the jokes about Branson being the place where old folks take their grandparents for vacation. But if you've never been to Branson, you've missed one of the most delightful vacation destinations in America. This "G Rated" town in the Ozarks is home to dozens of the best family entertainment venues anywhere. Whether your family is into amusement parks, horseback riding, shopping, or going to great stage shows, there's something for everyone in this quaint mountain town.

During the week I visited briefly with one of my favorite people, Dusty Rogers. You may recognize him as the son of the late Roy Rogers and Dale Evans. More than any son I have ever known, Dusty has made it his sacred duty to continue holding the torch high for his famous parents and what they stood for.

By the 1950s Roy Rogers was, by far, the biggest cowboy star in the world. A generation of baby boomers never missed one of his eighty-eight movies or any of his one hundred weekly TV episodes. There were Roy Rogers' records, comic books, clothes, and toys—in all, more than 400 licensed Roy Rogers' products. At his peak, he received well over 500,000 pieces of fan mail per month! Roy Rogers was, indeed, The King of the Cowboys.

But he was more than that. Roy was also a role model for millions of kids. For years, his and Dale's free time was filled making personal appearances and visiting children's hospitals. And everywhere the couple went they taught by word and example.

Being a baby boomer myself, it will come as no surprise that I am still a Roy Rogers' fan. My kids grew up hearing about and seeing Roy on a daily basis. There's an autographed poster of Roy in our Florida Room. There's an embroidered Roy Rogers cushion on the couch in the library. And in my office there's a full size Roy Rogers' cutout complete with his six-shooters drawn. Also in my office is a photograph of Roy and me backstage at a television show where he was appearing.

Lastly, hanging on the wall in our home is the "Roy Rogers Riders Rules." This was the ten-point manifesto to which all true Roy Rogers fans subscribed. I realize that this may sound like ancient history, as it was first produced back in the 1950s. But as I reread it after returning from Branson, I was taken aback by how profound, and still applicable, this little credo remains today. As you read it, ask yourself, "Doesn't this square with the Bible—and wouldn't it be a better world if today's parents (and grandparents) took a few minutes to relate the story of Roy Rogers and share these ten points with the children in their lives?"

1. Be neat and clean.
2. Be courteous and polite.
3. Always obey your parents.
4. Protect the weak and help them.
5. Be brave but never take chances.
6. Study hard and learn all you can.
7. Be kind to animals and take care of them.
8. Eat all your food and never waste any.
9. Love God and go to Sunday school.
10. Always respect our flag and our country.

"Wow, Steve," you may be thinking, "that's pretty corny stuff." I would agree. But who ever said that corny is bad? Maybe it's time for parents, grandparents, teachers, and coaches to stop allowing the culture to dictate the terms. Maybe it's time we stop allowing the inmates to run the asylum, and start reclaiming the cultural debate. Maybe it's time for those of us who still believe this sort of stuff to speak it more boldly than ever before.

It boils down to a pretty simple question. Which is more important: to look cool and go along to get along, or to take a stand that defies the drift of a society which seems bent on self destruction? Maybe your single candle in the cave would bring the light of hope and optimism that so many of our kids desperately need.

Postscript: I had every intention of ending this chapter with a shameless plug encouraging you to go to the Roy Rogers and Dales Evans Museum in Branson. But last evening I got an email that I didn't want to receive. It told me that, although Dusty and his show will continue performing in Branson, the museum will be closed by the time this book goes to press. I suppose it was inevitable. The generation that grew up loving Roy Rogers is aging. But here's the real question: Aren't the principles that Roy stood for perennial? What if we passed this same heritage on to those who follow us?

53

GIVE ULTIMATE PRAISE TO GOD

This I believe: When God blesses an individual, it becomes that person's responsibility to glorify God for that blessing. Over and over in the Bible, we read stories of how people went about rejoicing and telling others when Jesus healed them. This was one of the most effective ways to witness to the power of the gospel.

I believe it's the same today. So please forgive me for sharing a most personal story that I have never before written about. I'm doing this because I want you to know just how good and strong our God is.

As I've told you, in 1992 I had five heart bypasses at the ripe young age of thirty-nine. Thankfully, God brought healing. Over the years I changed my lifestyle, dropped weight, began a serious exercise program, and took all the required meds. However, by late 2000 I wasn't feeling very well. So I went back to the hospital for an arteriogram. I'll never forget the way the doctor began his meeting with Bonnie and me that afternoon. This top flight cardiologist looked at us and said, "This isn't going to be a very pleasant meeting." Then he commenced to tell me that, while my five bypasses were doing well, I had developed small artery disease. He explained that that meant the hundreds of small arteries that circle and feed my heart were clogging up. "Further," he explained, "they are too small for us to bypass. There's really nothing we can do. You may have a couple of years to live."

That, dear friend, was a hard day. I still remember, once out of the doctor's office, Bonnie crumpling into my arms. We were dazed. It's in moments like these that you know who your true friends are. I remember getting with Rubel Shelly, Mike Root, and Don Finto. Their prayers helped keep my head above water. We later learned that the news about my condition had gotten onto the internet and people were praying a twenty-four-hour vigil for me. We met with the elders of my church. I jokingly tell people that my leaders are the dumbest guys in the world. They don't try to figure God out—they just try to obey him. As James prescribed, they prayed over me and anointed me with oil.

One week later, Bon and I went back to the cardiologist for our follow up. Frankly, I don't remember why. Maybe it was so they could begin helping me prepare to die. But (and this is where it gets hard) that wasn't God's plan for our appointment. The doctor began by saying, "We've been studying and reviewing your arteriogram videos all week. It's as though, every time we put them back on the monitor, we see a new heart." He was, in essence, saying that my heart was healing itself! Although my doctor was an unbeliever, Bonnie and I knew the truth. He went on to say that the two- or three-year timeline was off the table. Although I was still a sick pup, I might live a good deal longer. Of course, it was understood that I had a progressive disease and that things wouldn't get better. In a few years I might not feel as well.

I praise God to tell you that, at this writing, it has now been nearly ten years. I have had two major follow up studies since November 2000—and in both cases my heart has actually improved! Today, I feel great! I regularly travel over 150 days yearly, often hauling a hundred pounds of gear through airports. And I go to the gym three days weekly where I run approximately five miles in under thirty-five minutes on a Stair Master. (Granted, I cheat a little bit by leaning on the handles.) But guess what? I'll bet my cardiologist couldn't keep up with me!

I don't tell you this story to brag. There is nothing special about me. I don't know why God elects to heal some people, and not heal others. In the Bible, some of the people God healed had faith, others didn't. Some appeared worthy, others didn't. As I discussed in "Remember Past Blessings," when our faith is under duress there's nothing like a reminder that God still works—up close and personal. This I do know: When God does a mighty work in your life, you have the obligation to tell others just how good, how strong, and how able your God is.

54

BE SLOW TO
JUDGE OTHERS

Let's talk tough. There is a time to call a sin a sin. And there are moments when, to please Jesus, we must do so. Sure, I know that's not a popular, or politically correct, comment—but it's true.

"Wait a minute," you protest, "didn't Jesus tell us not to judge others?"

You, dear friend, are right. He did. In Matthew, Jesus says, "Do not judge, or you too will be judged. For in the same way you judge others, you will be judged." But it is important to ask exactly what Jesus meant.

The Bible tells us that one day God will judge us all. So apparently Jesus didn't mean that we will never be judged. Could it also be that Jesus wasn't telling us *never* to judge either? Is it possible that what Jesus was teaching is the simple truth that it is wrong to have a harsh, hasty heart? You know the sort. This is the person who always seems ready to condemn and criticize others—without ever looking within his own soul. This is the sort of judgment where one mere mortal supposes to know the motives of another mortal. I used to be that sort of person. I was convinced that God and I were sort of co-judges. But as the years have passed, and I have become increasingly aware of my own failures, I am no longer in that part of the judging business.

However, I continue to believe that there is type of judging that I should do regularly. But it doesn't involve me focusing on the motivations of people's hearts—and condemning (or acquitting) them accordingly. Instead, it has more to do with discerning right and wrong. These days, I'm trying to run everything that I see through a single filter: Is this something that Jesus would smile at? If the answer is yes—then I go forward. If it's no, then I stop.

This means that when I see another person with whom I have a relationship doing wrong, love dictates that I speak to him about it. But by so doing, I'm not presuming to be the final judge—that's God's job. Instead, like a good fruit inspector, if I see something that looks wrong, I owe it to my friend to communicate my concerns. Let me share a few thoughts that have helped me determine when and how to do this.

- Be a Matthew 18 Christian. This is where Jesus gives instructions on how to approach a brother who is committing an offense. The most salient points are that we should do this in love; and we go to him in private. When you have a problem with someone else's behavior, don't talk to anyone but that person.
- Earn the right to speak candidly. This means that we should attempt to build a relationship *before* we dare to criticize. If I have never cared enough to invite someone into my home or to spend time conversing, isn't it pretty presumptive for me to speak to that person about something she is doing that I believe is wrong?
- Be slow to assume that the other person is being intentionally evil. Often the other person has never been taught a better way of doing things. Be patient.
- Be tolerant of the person. This isn't to be confused with being tolerant of his sin. Assume the best. Go to the person remembering that you, too, are vulnerable to sin.
- Be slow to pronounce another person's behavior as "sinful." Remember, Paul was very clear that sin is frequently a matter of conscience. If a certain behavior offends my conscience, then it is patently wrong for me to continue in that practice. But if

another Christian can do the same thing with a clear conscience before God, it may not be sinful for that person.

- Finally, allow God to do the convicting. The Bible tells us that one of the jobs of the Holy Spirit is to convict us of sin. Sometimes the best thing to do is pray that God will open another's heart to his conviction in their life.

55

REMEMBER THAT IT'S NEVER TOO LATE

D o you ever feel as if it's simply too late to get it together? You've failed so many times that there is no way home? Maybe your third marriage has just fallen apart. Possibly you've been fired for the second time in a year. Perhaps your relations with your relatives are nonexistent. You've promised God, "Never again!" But once more, you've returned to your drug of choice—be it alcohol, sex, drugs, or simply taking your maxed-out credit card back to the mall after promising your spouse that you wouldn't. Possibly, that one person who still trusted you has finally washed his hands and walked away. And in your heart of hearts you know that he is right: You've blown it—again.

Whatever your imperfection, please listen very carefully: It is never too late to begin doing the right thing.

Let that short sentence sink in. God is the God of the second and the one thousandth chance. No matter who you are, where you've been, what you've done, or who you've done it with—it is not too late to begin doing the right thing.

Christians and non-Christians alike tend to forget the second chance. "Sure," you agree, "God's forgiveness is real." But in your heart of hearts, you simply don't believe it's possible. Not for you. "How in a pull-myself-up-by-the-bootstraps, pay-as-I-go, and earn-my-own-keep world do I start over?

It's too late. I've hurt too many people. I've disappointed God too often. I'm a screw-up."

I'll admit that one cannot un-ring a bell. There may well be lasting scars and, possibly, things will never be fully healed in this earthly realm. But there is a victory to be won and it's yours for the taking if you are simply prepared to start doing the right thing right now. Thankfully, we have a God who is far less interested in our past behaviors than he is in what happens going forward.

As long as there is breath, and a will on your part, it is not too late to chart a new course. Some of history's greatest success stories were birthed in the gut of tragedy, failure, defeat, and sin. Wall Street tycoon Michael Milken epitomized the greed that defined the 1980s for many people. After a host of indictments, he eventually pled guilty to six securities and reporting violations. Upon leaving prison, Milken determined to begin doing the right thing. Today he uses his wealth to fund groundbreaking research for the cure of melanoma and other life threatening diseases.

I also think of Charles Colson. In the 1970s he went to prison for illegal and immoral behavior in the Nixon White House. Although his formal title was Special Counsel to the President, Colson was known as the "go to guy" for dirty tricks. After his guilty plea for obstruction of justice and a prison sentence, Chuck also determined to begin doing the right thing. In the decades since, he has worked tirelessly for the downtrodden. Colson's Prison Fellowship Ministry has given hope to thousands of hopeless people. In 1993 he was awarded the Templeton Prize. This honor is bestowed on one person annually who has done the most to advance the cause of religion. By the way, it is reported that Colson gave his million-plus dollar award to Prison Fellowship Ministry, as he does all his income from speaking and royalties.

If you are sick and tired of being sick and tired of being sick and tired, let me share three ideas that I believe you will find helpful.

1. Commit to God right here and now to trust him to be your righteousness. The fact is, you can't do it by yourself. Begin to

look to him for your inner strength. Seize the first opportunity that God gives you to begin doing the right thing. Then, with perseverance and tenacity, hold on and determine to continue doing good.

2. Make what's wrong right. By this, I mean do whatever is within your power to make things right. Apologize to those you have wronged. Pray for someone who won't accept your apology. Love others without requiring that they love you first. Trust God to make things right in relationships that you have no control over. Then, at night, pillow your head with a gentle smile as you picture that day in heaven when you and those you've struggled with here on earth fall into one another's arms with forgiveness and love. Be ready to forgive others. One thing that Jesus is incredibly clear about is that your sins will be forgiven based on the degree to which you elect to forgive those who have sinned against you. "And forgive us our debts, as we also have forgiven (left, remitted, and let go of the debts, and have given up resentment against) our debtors" (Matthew 6:12, The Amplified Bible).

So get busy. Find someone to forgive. Hold no grudges. Be an excessive, aggressive forgiver. Life is too short to do anything less.

56

LIVE IN THE REAL WORLD

Have you ever found yourself mesmerized staring at a computer screen saver? Maybe it's a starry sky or a mountain scene. My favorite is the aquarium with all the beautiful deep sea fish.

The desire to escape is most normal. We live in a trying and difficult world. And sometimes we want to escape to another place or time that seems happier. Whether it's a screen saver or a mind journey back to a simpler time, most of us dream of a place or time where things were "perfect." I suspect that this is one reason that nostalgia is so popular. Antique malls are filled with old 45 rpms, Shirley Temple dolls, and Coke memorabilia.

I'm not suggesting that there is anything wrong with remembering the past with a smile. I certainly do this myself. I love the decades of the 1950s and early 1960s. My own basement is a retro-room. Pictures cover the walls of various pop stars from that era who were interview guests on *Coast to Coast Gold*, the radio show I hosted over a decade ago. Even the furniture is retro—I have a sofa and love seat covered with aqua blue and hot pink funny fur. There's a lava lamp. I have a couple of Elvis autographs—and a picture of the two of us together. In the corner is my drum set—the same one I've played since the 1960s. And most of the music I play the drums to hails from that same era.

But there is a potential danger in all of this wistfulness. The danger comes when we sacrifice the "here and now" on the altar of "the good old days." When we strain our necks looking back at what has gone before, we miss the present. When we look for a "perfect" screen saver world, we will be disappointed. Granted, every fish on the screen saver floats dreamily past displaying its beautiful colors. The water is so blue you want to dive in for a swim. And there's nothing messy. None of that gross stuff on the bottom, no fish poop, and not a single fish floating upside down on the surface. It appears to be the perfect world.

The only trouble is, it's a lie. As you look for a happier time (whether, for you, it's an earlier era or a perfect screen saver world), you will gradually notice some chinks in the dream.

Having been in radio, I enjoy listening to good disc jockeys. One of the best-loved deejays of the early rock n' roll era was Cousin Brucie. His baritone pipes and great sense of humor led to a legendary run on WABC in New York. Today, "The Cuz" is in his seventies but his weekend show on XM is still a favorite for millions of fans of the fifties and sixties music. Recently I heard him do something that I thought was profound. A fifteen-year-old girl called his request line to ask for a song. As is his style, Cousin Brucie spent a few minutes talking with the girl. Near the end of their conversation, she said, "I sure wish I had lived in the 1950s."

The easiest thing for Brucie to have done would have been to let the comment go, and simply play the song. But he didn't. He realized that some fatherly advice was in order. So in a kind, but deliberate way the veteran jock said, "Don't ever say that." He went on to explain that things in the 1950s weren't perfect either. It's fun to go back and enjoy the good from that era. But the key to a joyful existence is to live in the present. This can be the most rewarding and challenging time in history.

It's the same with screen savers. The more you watch one, the less real it appears. You soon notice that you're watching the same fish making the same moves over and over again. And in fact, they actually don't look all that real to begin with. After a few minutes it becomes boring because you realize it's just so many 1s and 0s that reboot and repeat over and over again. Everything is static. Nothing ever changes or moves forward. It's a fake existence.

Sadly, many of us dream of a perfect world. Then when it doesn't materialize, we stop dreaming about the possibilities and opportunities of the present. We become convinced that joy has eluded us because we were born at the wrong time, into the wrong family, or with the wrong screen saver. The trouble with rose-colored glasses is that they gloss over a lot of blemishes.

The fact is, the world is not an easy place. Since the curse in the Garden of Eden humankind has been destined for struggle. If you expect everything to fit neatly into place, your life will be a most miserable existence. But if you see the big picture and learn to appreciate the threads of both good and bad events, one day you will look back on the tapestry of a life that is filled with color, dimension, purpose, and beauty.

57

REMEMBER: WORDS HAVE MEANING

In this life chapter, I want to share a single strategy that will help you make more friends, have less stress, and owe fewer apologies. This strategy is simple in the sense that's it's easy to understand, but it is a tough one for most of us to put into action. In a word, it has to do with how we use our words. As Tom Peters puts it, "There is far too much talk and too little do."

This is a most autobiographical book. Like so much else that I am sharing with you, this topic is a continual struggle for me. It always has been. I can still remember my dad's frustration more than forty years ago after I had said something totally inappropriate. He looked at me and said, "Steve, you know what they say about counting to ten before you speak? In your case, make it a hundred."

Friends, the fact is, words mean things. Our words shape the way others think about themselves and us. Words can build up or tear down. Words can inspire or demoralize. Jesus warned, "Every one of these careless words is going to come back to haunt you. There will be a time of Reckoning. Words are powerful; take them seriously. Words can be your salvation. Words can also be your damnation" (Matthew 12: 36-37, The Message).

Following are a few thought sparklers that I have found helpful in avoiding some of the vocal pitfalls along the way:

- Count your words. If you are conversing with one other person, in most cases, if you're talking more than fifty percent of the time, you're talking too much. If there are three of you, limit your talking to about a third of the conversation. And so on. Granted, it's a cliché, but there's truth in the reminder that God gave each of us one mouth and two ears. There should be a direct relationship between the amount we use each.

- It would be a better world if we made it a point to lead with our ears and follow with our tongues. When the other person is talking—listen. This is not the time to be planning your pithy response.

- Never say with ten words what can be as effectively said with five words. Brevity is almost always a gratefully received gift. People tend to listen most to those who speak the least.

- Season your words with salt. Words mean stuff. Select your words carefully. Use words that succinctly communicate the point and the passion of your meaning.

- Know thy audience. Don't try to impress others with your words. Words are for one purpose: communication. If you are not communicating clearly, you are using the wrong words.

- Remember that every gift is from God—including your tongue. Everything word we say should be examined. Does it help or hurt? Build up or tear down? Will this comment make another person's life better or worse?

- Lastly, remember that your words are your "tell." Gamblers all know that the key to winning a poker game often lies is watching for their opponent's "tell." This is the thing that the other guy does that betrays his strategy. Jesus said essentially the same thing about how our words are a window to what is going on inside our hearts. "For out of the overflow of the heart the mouth speaks. The good man brings good things out of the good stored up in him, and the evil man brings evil things out of the evil stored up in him" (Matthew 12:34b-35, NIV).

Words mean things. They give away who we are, what we believe, and what's going on inside our hearts. The more conserved, cautious, and considerate our words become, the more holy, happy, and helpful we will become. As the Bible says, "Do not let any unwholesome talk come out of your mouths, but only what is helpful for building others up according to their needs, that it may benefit those who listen" (Ephesians 4:29, NIV).

58

MAKE YOUR MARRIAGE LAST

We live in a disposable culture. Whenever something newer, flashier, or with a deeper tan comes along, we start thinking about upgrading. It amazes me how a small broken switch on my dashboard requires a whole new instrument panel. And when was the last time you saw a TV repairman?

Replacing stuff isn't too big of a deal. But what about relationships? What happens when what was once beautiful to you isn't so beautiful anymore? What about when your spouse becomes less appealing? Then what do you do?

This is when you need to redefine what is beautiful. It's when we change our vision. We determine to redevelop our perspective. Remember: Perception *is* reality. And the good news is that perception can be changed.

Earlier this year our oldest daughter was married. Megan and Michael honored us by requesting that the nuptials be held at our home and that I perform the ceremony. So, being a wise father, I decided to go to an expert for some tips on how to officiate the best ceremony possible. That expert was my son, Joshua, who is a minister at a large Houston church and thus has more than his share of marrying experience to his credit. He was kind enough to email me a ceremony that he had used before. Joshua suggested that I present Michael and Megan with three charges that, if remembered, will help them end where they began—deeply in love.

I took Joshua's advice and used his three charges—with a few embellishments of my own. As I was thinking about this life chapter, it occurred to me that these are three points that have the potential to breathe new life into any marriage—even those that are running low on gas. As a matter of fact, I would be a better husband to Bonnie if I reviewed these principles every now and again. Although the actual wording varied slightly, here is what the father of the bride said on that afternoon in May:

Charge #1: I charge you both to make Jesus your personal hero and the model for your home.

Michael, God's assignment to you is to love Megan just as Christ loves the church. "Husbands, love your wives, just as Christ loved the church and gave himself up for her to make her holy . . ." (Ephesians 5:25-26a NIV).

Be ready and willing to give all that you are and all that you have to take care of her. Be willing to give your time to listen to Megan. There are times that she is going to want to talk. Be willing to give your energy to Megan. She is going to need your help. Be willing to work hard and provide for Megan. It doesn't have to be extravagant. Just make sure she has something to eat, something to wear, and a safe place to call home. You are also the spiritual leader of this marriage and your new home. Pray daily and be in the Word. You can't be like Jesus to your wife unless you know Jesus yourself. Share the Word with Megan and model it to her. Show her honor and respect. Serve her.

Megan, God's assignment to you is to respect and submit to you husband, Michael. "Wives, submit to your husbands as to the Lord. For the husband is the head of the wife as Christ is the head of the church . . . . Now as the church submits to Christ, so also wives should submit to their husbands in everything" (Ephesians 5:22-24 NIV). Some people will tell you that you should only submit to Michael when you agree with him. But that's not submission. Submission is listening to and following Michael, even when you don't agree. When you respect and esteem him, he will thrive all the more as the godly leader of your home.

Charge #2: Make your spouse your standard of beauty.

If your spouse is tall, then make "tall" your standard of beauty. If you spouse is short, then make "short" your standard of beauty. Whatever your spouse is should become your standard of beauty from this moment on.

Today, you are both young and fit. But what happens if one of you isn't so fit one day? Congratulations! Your standard of beauty has changed. Don't look outside of your marriage to find your standard. If God in his grace allows, you are going to grow old and gray and wrinkled together. You'll see the age lines in one another's faces as beautiful markings of the decades you have lived and loved together.

If you decide today to make your spouse your standard of beauty, then even though you'll see the gray and the wrinkles, you will see beyond the age to the beauty of the human spirit that never grows old and you'll find each other more attractive than you do today.

Charge #3: Work hard to make your last day of marriage better than your first day of marriage.

Today, you start your marriage. You've worked hard to make this the perfect day. But one day your marriage will end. And it will end in one of three very different ways. Either at a graveside where one of you speaks fondly of the great years spent together or in a courthouse—or, most hopefully, hand-in-hand as your eyes widen as Jesus appears to take you to his home together forever.

Too many couples work hard to make their first day of marriage great, but fail to ensure that their last day is even better. Care for each other. Don't grow angry toward the other. Avoid resentments. Talk well about each other in public. And make love often. Confess your mistakes quickly. Be equally quick to forgive—and to forget.

And on that last day, you will be proud of your legacy.

59

STAY INSULATED, NOT ISOLATED

I remember a day several years ago when Cal Thomas, the conservative columnist and FOX commentator, and I were on the same venue. Cal made a great comment in his presentation that succinctly speaks the entire point of this life chapter. He said, "Every morning I get up and read two things—the *New York Times* and the Bible. That way, I get both sides of the story." The audience laughed, but Cal had made his point.

Since the earliest days of Christianity there has been a debate: Exactly how involved should Christians become in this present, temporal world? This is what led to the creation of early monastic societies where Christian people elected to remove themselves from the worldly influences around them. This is what prompted the Pilgrims to leave Europe in search of a New World where they could practice their faith as they believed God desired. It is what, in more recent years, has fueled the popularity of home schooling.

Being a Christian and living in this physical world is, at best, a tension-filled existence. On the one hand, we want to fix our minds on God and the heavenly home that awaits us. But on the other hand, there are bills to pay, diapers to change, bosses to placate, and soccer games to attend.

As I've mentioned elsewhere in this book (see "Be Generous With Money"), I believe that God wants us to enjoy the good things that he blesses us with in this world. Jesus went to parties. He had an active social calendar and a lot of friends. Jesus never suggested that his followers should be isolated from this world. But he prayed that his followers would be insulated from the evil of this world. "My prayer is not that you take them out of the world but that you protect them from the evil one" (John 17:15, NIV).

So how does this play out in our lives today? Succinctly put, it means that we should keep our eyes on the big picture. This world is not our home. We are just passing through. As the old gospel hymn says, "Our treasures are laid up somewhere beyond the blue."

But while the concept is easy enough to understand, it is hard to live. In his landmark book, *The Screwtape Letters*, C. S. Lewis writes a dialogue between Screwtape (Satan) and Wormwood (an apprentice demon who has been given his first new Christian convert, with instructions to reclaim him for Satan.) At one point Screwtape tells Wormwood to get his "client" out of his apartment and back on the busy city streets so he will hear the sounds of the buses and feel "the real world." Of course, Screwtape's goal is to get this new Christian to fall back into his old reality—and begin a drift away from Christ.

It's curious how, in the passage from John, Jesus never suggested that God remove his disciples from the world. If they had been allowed such a departure who would have been left to reach the unsaved masses? As a matter of fact, Jesus vehemently resisted this notion. Do you remember the mountain top experience when he was transfigured? There Jesus was with Moses and Elijah! What an overwhelming sight it must have been as Peter, James, and John looked on in amazement. Finally, Peter proclaimed that it would be a great idea to kick back, build some temples, and stay on top of the mountain. But Jesus wasn't interested in that idea. He knew that as great as that mountain-top experience was, the real work was on the streets below which were filled with hurting, broken, and lost people. Jesus essentially said, "Enough of this, it's time to get back to work." Maybe he realized that this experience would help to insulate his apostles from the vicious assaults of Satan, but he was determined not to allow it to isolate them from the very people who needed ministry.

But to impact the world around us positively we need to be prepared. The trick here is for Christians to understand what the "real world" actually is. This is why it would do many of us well to turn off the television, radio, and XM. It would be helpful to get away to the mountains or to the beach like Jesus did. It might be wise to schedule "quiet times" so we can hear the music of God over the noise of the world. The discipline of regular Bible study plays in here. It's only with this sort of spiritual fortification that we will be able to address the needs we see around us.

My nephew, David Clayton, is one of the most courageous young men I know. He is a Christian college chaplain. But his vision isn't limited to simply talking to kids who already know Jesus. David is determined to be insulated without ever becoming isolated. During spring break, David and a group of well-trained, well-taught, well-prayed (well-insulated) young men get out of their comfort zone and go to Florida. They go into bars where other young people are behaving badly. There's no frontal assault. Instead, David and his friends go in two-by-two and hang out drinking bottled water. They simply wait for God to offer them opportunities to minister. It's amazing how many lives have been touched by these young guys. They have shared Jesus with kids who were desperate—and reminded others (who were Christians) that what they were doing wasn't right.

The key: remembering that if we properly insulate ourselves, we will never want or need to isolate ourselves. What a remarkable way to share Jesus!

60

BE A CHEERLEADER

Have you ever said something and watched the words leave your mouth, then almost immediately wish you could pull them back before they hit the other person's ears? Recently that happened to me. I had concluded a speaking engagement where I had shown people how to save money buying cars. In the hallway a wonderful lady stepped up to me. She gleefully told me about how she had recently purchased a car and saved a lot of money. Thoughtlessly, I responded, "So did I. And I saved _____ (mentioning an amount that made her experience seem less important)." She was a good sport and gracious in her response, but I know she walked away emotionally bruised.

Immediately I regretted my childish, narcissistic response. Why had I done such a thing? Why did I feel as if I had to "prove" myself to her? What prompted me to "one-up" this sweet lady?

Maybe you have done the same thing. And, although you may have felt a momentary thrill by pinning someone else to the floor, you went away feeling badly about yourself. You regretted the boastfulness and the pride that led to such a bad choice.

I think there is a competitive tendency in many of us that prompts us to want to win the board game, beat the guy on the other side of the net, and generally dominate others in our circle of acquaintances. We want to impress others. We want glory. We want other people to know just how accomplished and pedigreed we are.

But it is a sweet moment when an individual finally stops insisting on being the center of the universe and allows (even encourages) others to bask in the lime light. If this is a battle for you, why not attack it and do differently? Actually, you could make it a game. Think of yourself as someone else's ambassador, promoter, or cheerleader.

The next time you go to a party or a social function, select someone whom you know is overworked and underappreciated. Then go up to that person and thank her for the good she has accomplished. Don't be artificial, but be gregarious enough to continue the conversation. Lean over and ask someone nearby if they know your friend's story. Or grab a couple by the arms and turn them around to face your friend. Continue by sharing with the growing crowd what this person has done or accomplished. Then encourage the person to tell you more. And while she is talking, avoid the temptation to interrupt with a story that features you. Instead, when she stops talking, prompt her by asking, "So then what happened?" Or, "Tell us more about how you accomplished that." I think you will be amazed on two levels. First, the person about whom you are bragging may be a bit embarrassed—but she will also be absolutely glowing. You will have honored her immensely. And second, you will walk away with a sense of joy that is much greater than you feel when you have made yourself the center of attention.

In the long run you will gain more honor (and likeability) when you help others gain respect. Not only will the person whose praises you sing love you, but others who witness your behavior will be inspired by it. They will gravitate towards you.

Before we hang up the phone on this chapter, let's get back to that nagging fault that I admitted to earlier: the desire to be the center of attention. How do we deal with this struggle? It begins by realizing that our value really doesn't come from within. Our value, abilities, and talents are all gifts from God. So we really have very little to brag about. The only truly appropriate emotion is humble gratitude.

Learning to be a team player is also helpful here. As a general rule, team players are better liked than self promoters. Ultimately all that really matters is how much good is accomplished. So it doesn't really matter who pushes the ball across the goal line. What matters is that the team scores. I still remember a little paper weight that someone gave me many years ago. There was a proverb on it to the effect, "There is no limit to what can be achieved as long as it doesn't matter who gets the credit." Learn to enjoy seeing others receive the attention and praise.

Also, remember that honor only counts when it comes from others. I don't need to be my own public relations factory. Wait for others to honor you. Jesus spoke of how counterintuitive God's way of doing things is. He was fond of saying that the "first will be last and the last will be first." He also advised that when you go to a banquet don't take the seat of honor lest your host ask you move to a back table. Instead, start out at the back table. Then when your host invites you to sit at the head table there will be true honor.

61

TURN YOUR WORLD
INTO A RAINBOW

In two other books, I've written at length about the concept of time management. And I have admitted to being a bit obsessive compulsive on the topic. Granted, there's a lot to be said for stopping to smell the roses. But in this chapter I want to bring a counterbalance to the suggestion that life is best spent in slow motion. Frankly, some of my greatest joy comes when I pillow my head knowing that the day has been a whirlwind of projects, people, and possibilities met. I like to accomplish stuff. I like to make the moments count.

In my earlier book, *Free to Succeed*, I wrote a chapter on time management called, "Managing Your Vanishing Inventory." The phrase "vanishing inventory" speaks to how precious and fleeting every tick of the clock is. In the broadcast business ad salesmen understand that they have a "vanishing inventory." In other words, every commercial slot that goes unsold is gone forever. That's why radio and TV stations frequently sell unsold commercial time at highly discounted rates just before it airs. It's the same in the hotel business. One of the best ways to get a great deal on a motel room is to pass several motels looking for the one with the fewest cars in the parking lot. Then quickly grab your Blackberry or log on at a Wi-Fi hotspot, and check their posted room rate. Suppose its $115. Then, armed with some knowledge, call that motel and ask for the desk manager. Tell him that you're in the area shopping for a good motel rate. Then ask, "Could you sell me a room for tonight for $80?" Realizing that potential revenue from any rooms he doesn't rent in the next few hours is gone forever, he may agree to your offer. If not, you're still likely to rent the room for well under the $115 on-line rate.

It's equally important for individuals like you and me to manage our vanishing inventory of time. This is where effective time management comes into the equation. Lots has been written and taught on the topic, but in this chapter I want to share one quick, simple, and very doable idea that will help you manage your time and balance your life.

This is an idea that Bonnie (who learned about it from one of her friends) recently shared with me. Bonnie and her friend use this little technique to be certain that they don't allow anything to absorb a disproportionate amount of their day. Here's how it works.

Why not color-code your life? This little technique works equally well whether you keep your schedule on a smart phone, your computer, or on an old-fashioned, handwritten appointment book. Simply divide your activities into various categories. Then select a color for each category. You can accomplish this either by using a different ink (or font) color for each activity or by printing everything in black and then using different highlighters to color the varying tasks. Some of the headings in your breakdown might include:

- Time with children
- Time with husband/wife
- Time in Bible study
- Time at the gym
- Time visiting friends
- Time given to others (benevolence, cleaning a home for a widow, time with a fatherless child, volunteer efforts, etc.)
- Other (This will vary depending on your age, commitments, involvements, etc.)

Then assign a different color to each topic. Once you have your week's schedule prepared, look at it as a whole. What does it look like? Is it a boring monotone? Are you looking at pretty much the same two or three colors everywhere? Or is it a kaleidoscope of shades, all mixed together into a diverse and intriguing blend of beautiful colors?

I believe that if you will try this little strategy, several good things will happen. First, you will immediately know when your life is getting out of balance. Then you can make the needed adjustments before there are consequences. Second, you will avoid the boredom of becoming stuck in a rut doing the same monotonous activity sequentially. We tend to become less productive when we become fatigued. And fatigue sets in when we don't permit ourselves to change tasks as the day progresses. And finally, you will find a new balance in your life. This little technique will help you avoid spending too much time doing any one thing to the exclusion of other equally important things.

62

DON'T BE A "HAMSTER CHRISTIAN"

Most religion doesn't work. Why? Because most religious belief systems are built on a false premise that is destined to fail and leave the follower overwhelmed, disillusioned, and disenfranchised. This is why so many religious people eventually give up and stop trying.

What is this most destructive of all religious beliefs? It's the belief that we can be good enough to gain God's love and acceptance. It's the notion that an individual can do something that will earn God's favor. When you stop to think about it, this is what most religions throughout history have been based on. Pagans practiced self mutilation and sacrificed their children all to appease their deities. Muslims have a belief system based on their works. And sadly, many Christians have fallen into a similar belief system. This is why some Christians go through life believing, "Once saved—always in doubt." This explains why there are Christians who believe that one day God is going to judge them by comparing the number of good deeds to bad deeds that they have done. This is why many Christians have misunderstood grace—and actually believe that their good works determine their salvation.

When we believe this lie we set ourselves up for failure. We become hamster Christians. Have you ever watched a hamster running on a wheel? He stays busy—but never gets anywhere. This is how far too many Christians spend their lives. We're always running and trying to do enough good things to win God's favor. Yet because we are sinners, we always come up short. It's little wonder many of us aren't excited about Jesus—and in no hurry to share him with our friends.

Over and over again in Scripture we are told that salvation is a gift of God's grace. Granted, he doesn't force his grace on non-receptive people. One certainly must be willing to accept Jesus as his personal savior. But considering any responsive action as a "work" is similar to a seventeen-year-old whose dad buys her a car. Dad points at the kitchen table and says, "There are the keys, enjoy your car." Wouldn't it then be ridiculous and arrogant if that young woman began bragging to her friends that she had worked to earn her new car simply because she had reached out her hand to pick up the keys? That would not be considered work. That would be considered the acceptance of a free gift.

There is a reason why humanity insists on working its way to God. It's because there is a demonically influenced nature within us that leads us to want to be our own gods. We want to feel as if we control our own destiny. We want to be the captain of our lives. We want to have enough god within ourselves to deal with God on an equal footing. And in a way this makes sense. After all, we live in a world where we have to prove our worth by paying for whatever we get. We are judged on our performance. And this is all fine in the job market or the classroom. But when we begin to deal with Jehovah God this way, we have missed the mark.

This has always been a problem for us humans. Paul had to tell the Ephesians over and over (you'll count four times in the following verse alone) that they were saved by God's grace: (1) "For by grace you have been saved through faith; (2) and that not of yourselves, (3) it is the gift of God; (4) not as a result of works, so that no one may boast" (2:8-10, NASV).

So it's fair to ask, "What about works? Don't works have a place in the Christian's life?" My answer (as was Paul's) is an emphatic, YES! But not in the sense many Christians believe. Actually, Paul lays out his belief system concerning works in the next verse. "For we are His workmanship, created in Christ Jesus *for* good works, which God prepared beforehand so that we would walk in them."

Notice the little word "for" in the above passage. That's a very important word. It comes from a Greek word that means exactly what it says: "for."The trouble is, some of us read this passage as though it says that we are created in Christ Jesus *because* of our good works. Do you see what that does to one's theology? If we are saved "because" of our good works, we're suddenly back on that hamster wheel running for all we're worth trying to do enough good works to get (or stay) saved. That is heresy! And that is what causes many Christians to finally give up in frustration.

When we finally understand the concept of salvation by grace alone, there won't be enough power on the planet to keep us from doing good works. Not to get saved—but because we *are* saved.

63

DO IT TODAY

It seems that the slogan for today's culture is, "Tomorrow is today's greatest work-saving device."

Fact: that's not true!

However, we live in a world filled with procrastinators. It is tough to get a handyman to hang a door. It's hard to get some people to return our phone calls. It is nearly impossible to get a plumber in a hurry. Procrastination is a dangerous bed fellow. The trouble with putting off until tomorrow what should be done today is that tomorrow may never come. No matter how daunting a job is, the best way to get it done is to begin. Popular motivational speaker, Alyce Cornyn-Selby says, "Procrastination is, hands down, our favorite form of self sabotage." I am convinced that more personal failure is the result of procrastination than a lack of know-how, intelligence, opportunity, and ability combined. Procrastination dooms a person's hope for success.

It's been said that procrastination is suicide on the installment plan. Beating procrastination is all about coming to a moment in one's life when instant gratification finally takes a backseat to doing what is right for the long-term. It involves learning to see the big picture. If you surveyed the top businesspeople, pro athletes, and sales teams, they would all have at least one thing in common. They would tell you that the key to success is doing what needs to be done *when* it needs to be done.

There are plenty of practical things you can do to address this issue. For instance, the best way to end any day is by doing a "to do" list for the next day. Don't go to bed until you know what you will be doing tomorrow. Once you have made that list put a number beside each task. Make #1 the job you least want to do. Then, when morning arrives, get up and do that job first. The rest of the day will be an easier downhill slide.

But to truly overcome procrastination we must go beyond mere mechanics. There also must be a rock solid conviction that procrastination is harmful and wrong. People who procrastinate let other people down. They let themselves down. And most importantly, they let God down. Procrastination, by definition, is leaving important things undone while things of less importance are allowed to fill our time.

I recently heard a Christian teacher make a strong case for the damage that procrastination can cause into eternity. He shared the story of Felix and his wife Drusilla as it is reported in Acts 24. (You might want to take a few minutes and read this most interesting chapter.) Paul first met this couple as a prisoner. He was called before them to make his defense of Christianity. Felix was governor in Palestine. He knew Jews and their customs. In the tradition of great lawyers through the ages, the prosecuting attorney, Tertullus, begins this chapter with hyperbole to curry favor with Felix. But despite Tertullus' glowing rendition of the governor's accomplishments, in truth Felix had been a tyrant of the first order who was on his third marriage. His contemporaries referred to Felix as a man who indulged in "every kind of barbarity and lust." His wife, Drusilla, was of Jewish heritage. But she was apparently following in the footsteps of her extended family. Drusilla's family tree was responsible for the beheading of John the Baptist, the attempted murder of Peter, and the killing of Jewish babies at the birth of Jesus.

Talk about a tough audience—Paul's work was cut out for him. But he was up to the task. According to the Bible, Paul spoke poignantly about "righteousness, self control, and the judgment that is to come."

One would hope that such a convicting sermon would prove to be a turning point for Felix and Drusilla. But, oh no! The monster of procrastination set into Felix's heart as he declared, "That's enough for now! You may leave. When I find it convenient, I will send for you." Trouble is, like most procrastinators, Felix apparently never found his "more convenient time." And it cost him his soul.

Life is too short to spend it putting off until tomorrow what should be done today. If there is a job that needs to be done today, get busy. If there is a kindness that you can do, do it now. If there's an apology that you owe, make it before the sun sets. If there is a "Thank you" to be said, get with it.

In the words of the old Bill Gaither song, ". . . the Father may be standing up right now, to give the call, to end it all. So keep on walking."

64

PROVIDE EMOTIONAL STROKES TO OTHERS

This morning was a good morning. Bonnie and I both woke up early. Since neither of us had to rush into the day, we simply lay side by side in the bed holding hands saying important things to one another. She told me how much she loves me and that I am still her best friend. I told her how much I love and respect her. We made our moments and words count. I call these emotional strokes. A couple of hours later she dropped me off at the airport with a kiss, a prayer, and some more emotional strokes. Right now the plane isn't the only reason that I'm flying high.

Over the years I've heard the same things you have about how it takes at least twenty (or was that seventeen?) kind comments to undo one negative remark. Kind comments feel good. Unkind comments hurt. So, if kind comments are a good thing, let me ask you a question. Can you remember the last time someone approached you to speak a warm, sincere, heartfelt compliment? I suspect your answer will be one of two. Either you will have to sadly say no. Or you will say yes. But, if you do say yes, let me ask another question. Did you say yes because that compliment was such a rare occurrence that it still stands out in your memory?

Granted, we can't control how others speak to us, be we can control how we chose to speak to others. So why don't we do a better job sharing emotional strokes—speaking words of kindness and encouragement to others?

Sometimes it's because of misconceptions on our part. For instance, I used to believe that this was a girl thing. I thought women needed more emotional strokes than we guys. I don't believe that anymore. To their credit, women seem to give and receive more emotional strokes. But I'm increasingly convinced that guys need emotional stoking at least as much as women. We men have fragile egos. Sure, we put on stoic facades, but inside most of us are still little boys who desperately need approval, affirmation, and affection.

Another reason we are too sparing with our emotional strokes is because we incorrectly assume that the other person is already aware of how we feel. Do you remember the old joke about the elderly wife who complained to her husband that in forty years of marriage he had never once told her that he loved her? With a stunned look on his face he said, "I told you that I loved you on our wedding day. If I ever change my mind, I'll let you know."

False humility and self centeredness keep some of us from sharing emotional strokes with others. Some people resist speaking a positive word to another person because, "I would be embarrassed." Or, "She would think I sound stupid." Or, "The other person might blow me off and be dismissive." When you think about it, all of these "reasons" are excuses resulting from too much focus on one's self. Certainly, some people will seem dismissive. But often those are the very people who need your emotional stroking the most. They are likely to be the people who get the fewest strokes—and least know how to accept one in a gracious manner. It's your job to give them some practice! It's a safe bet that virtually everyone you ever share an emotional stroke with is a person who dreams of being appreciated and recognized. After all, don't you?

Let me leave you with a few closing thoughts as I wrap this chapter up.

Becoming an emotional stroke giver is a learned skill. It may not come easy for you—especially if you tend to be shy and introverted. But with enough effort it will become a natural behavior. And the rewards are huge. The look in another person's face, and the way she will almost walk on air, will make your efforts very rewarding.

Don't limit you emotional strokes to just the people you live, hang, or work with. Be generous. Share your strokes with total strangers. You never know what burdens the checkout clerk or the pizza delivery guy is carrying. If there is a real, sincere, kind comment, make it.

Lastly, share lots of emotional strokes because Jesus wants you to do so. Think about it. Didn't Jesus tell us to treat other folk the way we would like to be treated? Personally, I like it when someone gives me an emotional stroke. So doesn't it follow that I should be aggressively sharing them with others? Wouldn't this be a wonderful way to return civility to an increasingly coarse and uncivil culture?

I started this visit by telling you about some of the emotional stroking between Bonnie and me. So far it's paid real dividends. We just celebrated our thirty-third anniversary—and she picked up my option for another two years.

65

BE A GENEROUS PERSON

Let me share a true, modern-day parable with you. There once was a father. He was a good man but he believed that most other people were out to get him. This false notion robbed him of a lot of peace. He tilted towards paranoia. He distrusted others. This made him resentful of things that most people were not troubled by. For instance, he didn't like to tip. When he went to a restaurant he was cheap. It was painful watching him dole out change to pay the servers. His theory was that the employers should pay their people enough so that tipping wasn't expected. Not only did this hurt his witness, it also inspired his son to be the same way.

Once an adult, his son for many years parroted what he had witnessed growing up. He too was cheap. He was openly resentful of people who expected gratuities. He disliked being asked to give anything extra to anyone. One day, while he was still a young man, the son hailed a taxi. At the end of the ride he handed the cabbie a large bill and insisted that every penny that hadn't registered on the meter be returned. The cab driver was angry and offended. But the young man saw nothing wrong with his behavior. He reported the cab driver's behavior to his father who consoled his son by confirming that his son was in the right and that the driver was in the wrong.

One day, perhaps by divine appointment, a light turned on in the son's head. He realized: This is wrong. It goes against all that is right and fair. If he was going to use the services of someone who depended on tips to survive, then it was wrong not to pay the tips. As a matter of fact, in time, he gradually realized that, since he was blessed financially (at least more than most of the people whose services he consumed), it was right and good to share what he had. As the years passed the son found more and more ways to share with other people. Also as the years passed, the son noticed something else. He realized that the miserly existence that his father had experienced was not worth the few extra dollars with which he died. Instead, the son found great joy in giving—sometimes to people who had no expectation of receiving.

It sort of became a hobby. One cold night he went into a convenience store and saw a man without a coat. The son pulled his leather jacket off and gave it to the man. Not only was the man blessed, but the son's children who were watching through the window from the car were impacted. That night that family's tree began to change. As the son's children grew up they remembered such examples of their father's generosity. They grew up to be givers themselves. None became rich—but all became happy.

If you haven't already guessed it, in this chapter I want to encourage you to be generous towards those who have less power and clout than you do.

There is a special joy that comes to one's life when one decides to become generous. Suddenly a lot of the pettiness of life dissipates. Much of the paranoia goes away. The fear that someone else will "win" and we will "lose" dispels. And life, in general, becomes more fun.

Why not look for golden opportunities for generosity? Instead of fifteen percent, why not occasionally surprise your server with a thirty percent tip? Why not leave ten or fifteen dollars on the desk before you leave the hotel? Why not give the shoeshine guy two dollars extra? Why not hand the grocery boy a couple of dollars when he puts the bags in your backseat?

Yes, it will bless the other person. But the greatest blessing will come to you. What we *give* we tend to *get* in return. If we give to others, we tend to cross-pollinate the culture. Others are happier, and so are we. Jesus told us that if we give, it will be given back to us—pressed down, shaken together, and running over. This isn't necessarily to say that other people will give you a wheelbarrow full of money just because you have learned to tip. But it does mean that God will fill your life with whatever your needs are. He knows you better than your fingerprints. And when he sees you sharing with others, it stands to reason that he will trust you with more of his stuff. Jesus told us that, "Whoever does it unto the least of these does it unto me."

And one more thing before I end this visit: Let me suggest that you give the credit to Jesus. What does that mean? It means that you give spiritual legs to your gift. When you leave the tip at the restaurant, why not say, "God bless you," as the server picks it up? Why not leave a handwritten note in the motel with a Scripture reference next to your ten or fifteen dollar tip? Why not spend a moment mentioning Jesus to the shoeshine guy before you hand him the extra two dollars? This way we extend the benefit of our tipping. It goes from being simply a physical blessing to becoming an eternal blessing.

66

LEARN TO COMPARTMENTALIZE

We've all heard the old show song, "There's No Business Like Show Business." In part, the lyrics talk about the way performers often "smile when they are low." In another verse the song intones, "Let's go on with the show."

While I would question whether a show is as important as the song suggests, I do like the stoic, get-it-done attitude that the song promotes. Pros are people who learn to see the big picture and do something about it. They learn to leave their personal concerns at the door.

One trait that is common among successful people is this ability to lay their personal baggage down and focus on a higher calling. Over the years I have known and worked with a number of business people, entertainers, and ministers who have developed this discipline. I call it the art of compartmentalization. In a nutshell, this is the ability to be a pro. It involves growing an emotional spine and not taking the course of least resistance. This is a learned talent. It involves being able to temporarily lay aside personal issues and worries in order to focus on a greater or more urgent problem. It is what the best athletes all learn to do. It is the mettle, grit, and resolve that separates leaders from followers. It is the courage required for a general to send troops into battle knowing that his own son will be on the front line. It is what the best leaders all learn to do.

There are times in each of our lives when we must decide whether to be driven by the passions and emotions around us or to focus resolutely on the task at hand. These are difficult moments. They happen in the most personal and private corners of our hearts—out of the view of other people. These are the times when we leave our private concerns at the door for the greater good. Athletes call this "putting on their game face."

If you hope to achieve true success in life, you must learn to compartmentalize. Whatever is going on in your private world—don't bring it into your professional world. Don't use a fight with your wife as an excuse to blow a presentation on the job. Don't permit the person who cut you off in traffic to become an excuse to mistreat one of your children. Don't allow worry about a negative doctor's report to keep you from serving another person's need.

In writing this I realize that some people may misunderstand my point and accuse me of promoting hypocrisy. That is not the case. Developing the talent of compartmentalization is not done to deceive or abuse others. It should be developed to help us focus less on selfish, personal needs—and more on the needs of others. This is actually the most pure form of love. Jesus told his followers to keep their private lives private. "When you fast, do not look somber as the hypocrites do, for they disfigure their faces to show men they are fasting . . . . But when you fast, put oil on your head and wash your face, so that it will not be obvious to men that you are fasting, but only to your Father" (Matthew 6: 16-18, NIV).

Compartmentalization means that one literally forgets one's own self and focuses, instead, on other people or duties that must come first. It involves rising above self absorption and doing what is best for the group.

People who grow to this level of personal and spiritual maturity are the ones who bless others the most—and are remembered most fondly. These are the people who realize that life is short and all that matters in eternity is the good we do for others.

67

RESPECT YOURSELF

Respect is one of those words that conjure up all sorts of mind pictures. You may think of a military salute, or saying "Yes, Ma'am" to your teacher, or obeying a roadside speed sign. But in this chapter I want to focus on a concept that is most difficult for some of us. Let's share a few thoughts about self respect.

The fact is, it is nearly impossible to have respect for others without first having respect for oneself. The degree to which you respect yourself will directly impact the way you love, honor, and respect other people. On various occasions Jesus told his followers to love others as they loved themselves. This command presupposes that one already *does* love oneself. Self love and self respect are inseparable twins.

Self respect begins with an important concept: the realization that every one of us has what some people call the "God particle." Since various people mean different things when using this term, allow me to define it as I mean it. I certainly am not suggesting that we are all gods. We are not. New agers and various cultists have long postulated that every human being is a god. This is heretical. And in fact, such a belief system destroys one's legitimate right to possess self respect. Why? Because if, despite all my sins and failures, I am still god—what does that say about the nature of a god?

The "God particle" that I refer to is that spark of the holy that God puts within each of us. When God first stepped into time and space and created humankind, he said, "Let us make man in our image, in our likeness . . ." (Genesis 1:26b, NIV).

When we realize that each of us has this "God particle," then the things of this world become less and less important. Gradually we see the accumulation of more stuff, our sexual conquests, and the power we wield over others for what it is—a poor substitute for true self respect.

Self respect begins with a growing awareness that God made you special. He has given you a very specific skill set that he hopes you will use, develop, and redeem for his glory. The more effectively we do this, the more self respect we will have. Comparisons to others will become less and less important. We will understand that we don't have to imitate what other people do. We will learn to appreciate our individualism and uniqueness as the gifts they are. And we will find joy in becoming what God designed us to be. This is why it is important never to allow the opinions of others to define who we are or how we feel about ourselves.

It may come as a surprise, but did you know that God actually endorses a certain form of pride? Paul told the Christians in the young Galatian church, "Each one should test his own actions. Then he can take pride in himself, without comparing himself to somebody else, for each one should carry his own load" (Galatians 6:4-5, NIV).

It is most appropriate to take a healthy pride in what you do and what you accomplish. The degree to which you develop and use your God-given skills is a direct reflection of how much you appreciate the gifts that God gave you. If you make the most of them, you will never·need to be jealous of persons or disappointed that you haven't achieved what someone else has. This is when you will be able to relax in the sweet spot of God's grace and bask in his love for you.

None of us were born to fail. God wants us to succeed. But to do so we must understand that God's definition of success and the world's definition of success are often very different. Self respect comes when you learn what God wants from you, and then strive for that godly success in your life.

Your level of self respect will directly impact your respect for others. It is difficult to show respect to others if you don't first have a healthy self respect. And conversely, as you extend more sincere respect to others, your level of self respect will increase. This means that we need to look aggressively for the good (the "God particle") in other people. Even those who show very little of it are still deserving of our respect simply because God loves and values them.

68

AVOID CUT AND PASTE THEOLOGY

D o you ever find the Bible confusing? Sometimes even two equally well-trained Bible scholars often come to diametrically opposed conclusions on the same topic. And have you sometimes wondered if the Bible actually contradicts itself?

These questions used to plague me. But in recent years some important concepts have come into better focus. Various writers like Lee Strobel and Rubel Shelly have made compelling presentations on how the Bible—although written as sixty-six separate books, over more than 1,500 years, by about forty different authors, from numerous countries—has a beautiful harmony and symmetry. The Bible is a book that harmonizes with itself and links logically with the physical world that we see around us. While never intended to be a science textbook, many of the Old Testament laws and teachings differed radically from the superstitions prevalent in pagan religions of those days. Today, many of the laws first presented by God to his people regarding sanitation and food preparation are the norm for anyone who wants to live a healthy life. The laws of equity that God laid out for his people have stood the test of time. Today, much of the free world's legal system is founded on the Judeo-Christian ethic. The concept of property rights, which God ordained, remains a cornerstone of contemporary Western culture.

So, why is there also so much argument, debate, and outright hostility over "what the Bible says?"

I believe it's because of what I like to call "cut and paste theology." This is when a person misuses the Bible to advance a personal agenda. This is when we approach the Bible with our minds made up; and then we selectively use Scripture fragments to push our pet points and promote our personal agendas. This is when we get lost in the religious weeds. It plays out in all sorts of ways on all sorts of topics. By picking and choosing which Scripture snippets they use, people have made forceful cases for all sorts of bizarre notions. Faulty methods of interpretation (or "cut and paste theology") have led some people to suggest that it is appropriate to be baptized for dead people; that slavery is God-ordained; and that polygamy is appropriate.

One of the most dangerous and intellectually dishonest things a Christian can do is use the Bible as his own personal bludgeon to browbeat another person. But far too many religious types do that very thing with moral abandon. Anytime someone uses the Bible to advance his own preconceived agenda, he or she becomes a dangerous person. The Bible is the final arbiter of God's will for humankind. But no one should develop his own belief system and *then* go to the Bible to "prove" it. Beware of anyone who attempts to justify a belief system by cutting a verse here and pasting one there.

The facts are these: The Bible was not written for our private interpretations. It should be taken as a whole. It is not my own personal hammer to beat up other believers—many of whom love God as much as I do.

I grew up in a world of rule-keeping religion which resulted in great anxiety. Being a Christian was more pain than pleasure. As the years passed I allowed my own misery to spill over onto others. I began to secretly enjoy beating other people up with my Bible. Thankfully, those days are passed. Today, I see God in a different way. I view the Bible differently, too. As someone has pointed out correctly, the Bible is actually far less of a rule book and far more of a love letter than many of us would believe possible.

I've never signed anyone's creed and I'm not planning to. Why? Because, on some matters, what I believe today is not what I believed five years ago. And I suppose that if God allows me to live a few more years, I'll probably change my thinking on more things. It's amazing how sometimes I'll go to a passage that I may have already read many times, yet God's Spirit will open my eyes to something brand new—a sparkling fresh vista that I've never seen in that passage before. God's Word really does live up to its billing: It's living and active and "sharper than any two edged sword" because it pierces my heart at levels that no human ever could. It convicts, it reassures, it redirects, and it promises a bright future.

So to restate my point: Don't reduce the Bible to your own personal proof text. Take it as a whole. Don't cut and paste together an odd or narrow theology. When you use the Bible as it is designed to be used, some cool things will begin to happen in your life. You will find a renewed joy in the Word. You will find yourself getting up a little earlier so you will have more time listening to God. When a person comes to the Bible as an empty, thirsty seeker, he will go away filled with God's Spirit—and discover the big picture.

69

KEEP SECRETS

O ver the years lots of people have told me lots of stuff. Some of these conversations were profoundly intimate and brutally honest moments. Some involved spiritual battles. Some dealt with marital unfaithfulness. Some focused on deep-seated worries. Some were about illnesses that others were not aware of. Some literally dealt with life and death issues.

One thing I like about me is that I have kept a lot of that stuff confidential. One thing I dislike about me is that sometimes I haven't.

When someone comes to you with a heavy heart and discloses something very personal, it's a safe bet that the other person is in a lot of emotional turmoil.

Usually when another person shares a confidence with you, what is being shared falls into one of two broad categories: It is either a fear that he has, or it is a sin that he is struggling with. The Bible says, "He who conceals his sins does not prosper, but whoever confesses and renounces them finds mercy. Blessed is the man who always fears the LORD, but he who hardens his heart falls into trouble" (Proverbs 28:13-14, NIV). Confession is truly good for the soul—but only when it is done in the safe harbor of confidentiality.

One of the highest honors you will ever receive is to be invited into another person's heart to share an intimate moment of this sort. So it is important that you understand the dynamic of what is happening—and that you handle it correctly.

Sometimes the other person needs your advice. But often what is most needed is a kind, sympathetic heart that is willing to listen, empathize, and be truly relational. Simply talking with you may bring all the cathartic relief that the other person desperately needs.

After the conversation is over—it then becomes your job to be certain that the conversation *really* is over. It is your duty to zip your lip and keep the secret. One of the most dishonoring ways to treat the other person (who has poured her heart out believing that you were a safe person with whom to speak) is to share any part of that confidential conversation with someone else. (Obviously, it goes without being said, that there may be rare exceptions to this rule. If this is a crime, or the person is going to harm herself or someone else, usually the loving thing to do is to inform the appropriate authorities.)

But as a rule, if you are a godly person, you will not betray the confidences of others. Godly people keep secrets. When that other person talked with you, he was demonstrating trust in you. It's likely that he was also hurting, felt guilty, needed a friend, and was in an emotionally vulnerable state. It was an intimate and very private occurrence.

God puts a high premium on keeping secrets. He tells us, "A gossip betrays a confidence; so avoid a man who talks too much" (Proverbs 20:19, NIV).

Most of the people in my life fall into one of three categories:

1. People I may like but don't trust. There are lots of people
   like this. I have friendly relationships with these people, but I
   would never dream of taking them into my confidence because
   whatever I might tell them would not remain confidential.
2. People with whom I might share a personal story—but only a
   semi-personal one. These are the people whom I trust a little
   bit. These are the people whom I make promise that "you
   won't tell anyone else" before I confide in them.

3. People whom I would trust with any secret. Fortunately, I
   know a number of people who fall into this category. I quickly
   think of my wife, our kids, and a number of close friends.

But the real focus of this chapter is introspective. Rather than attempting to tell you how to find such a confidant, my purpose here is to encourage you to *become* such a confidant. The world needs more trustworthy people. I'm convinced that one of the best ways to have a strong Christian witness is to be a secret keeper. One of the most effective ways to monitor your progress in this arena is to pay attention to how many people decide (or don't decide) to bring you into their confidence. If others don't seek you out to talk candidly and confidentially, don't get mad at them. Get real with yourself. Make the needed changes. The next time someone does share something private with you, do two things: Assure that person that the conversation will remain just between the two of you; and then, keep your word.

Let me suggest a goal: Make up your mind to die with a lot of secrets.

70

SET REASONABLE GOALS

Philosopher Bertrand Russell warned that we shouldn't mistake wishes for facts.

Throughout this book, I share a lot of advice. But, taken out of context, any one of the chapters may leave you with a skewed or incomplete picture. So please read this book as a whole. Simply stated, for one to *get* the big picture, one must first *see* the full picture. I have encouraged you to strive for excellence and perform at maximum capacity. I really believe in this principle. Unless one aims high, one will likely never achieve great things. My goal is to help you to go to your grave with the fewest possible regrets.

But it is also fair to remember that high expectations can become an individual's undoing. If lofty goals simply help us push a little harder, go the extra mile, and burn a little extra midnight oil—all in the quest of an attainable goal—that's a good thing. But if I allow unrealistic goals to become obsessions that leave me derailed, defeated, and demoralized when I miss one, that's a bad thing.

So, as I've tried to do throughout this book, I assert: Approach life with a balanced view. To accomplish this we should develop goals that inspire us to perform at our best. But if we use those goals as excuses to crawl over other people to get what we want, that's not good. If we allow a healthy ambition to achieve excellence lead us to a perfectionist lifestyle, we only end up harming ourselves and undermining the joy we should experience in the level of success that we *do* achieve.

There is a place for mental hyperbole. This is when we psyche ourselves up, and grunt, and beat our chests, and proclaim "I can do this!" But this should be seen for what it is: self motivation. All successful people understand the benefit of this behavior. This sort of "self talk" can supply the extra push and adrenalin rush that has helped countless people achieve far more than their equally talented (but less motivated) contemporaries will ever achieve. As you know, I am a huge believer in this sort of personal motivation.

But in fact, we can do ourselves a true disservice when such chest beating assurance is totally unrealistic. Let me explain what I mean. Suppose a young man in high school tops out at only 5'6". Now, let's suppose that his dream is to play competitive basketball. The problem is, he goes to a large high school and everyone on the team is at least 6'2". The young athlete's friends all laugh when he mentions his interest in playing for the varsity team. Even the coach is discouraging. But through sheer will, perseverance, and hundreds of extra hours of practice, it is conceivable that this young man might actually make the team and put in some serious game time. Yet there comes a point when this young guy must look himself in the mirror and get real with himself. He must admit the truth that he should not invest his physical and emotional energy (and his sense of self worth) in the goal of becoming a point guard for the Chicago Bulls. To do this will cripple him and leave him emotionally debilitated. If he invests all his energy in this unrealistic goal, he is likely to sacrifice a good college education and relationships with others. He is likely to end up with a lot of wasted effort and little to show for it. One day he will look around and realize that he has few friends, an inadequate education for his future, and a general sense of personal failure.

So here are my suggestions:

- Set reasonable goals. Be sure that they will force you to stretch— but not break.

- Be prepared to settle for less. As the old saying goes, "Shoot for the stars. Then, even if you only hit the moon, you will have done well."
- Understand that your achievements do not define your self worth. Before God, we all are at eye level. Your value is based upon the way you accept and reflect God in your life.
- Understand that your talents (or lack of certain talents) has nothing to do with your value before God. When it comes to the distribution of talent, God determines who gets what. Your only requirement is to redeem the talents that God has given you as fully as possible.
- If you are a perfectionist—stop! Perfectionism is the evil step-brother of laziness. Neither one is a productive way to spend one's life.
- Your value is not based upon what you do. It is based upon Who you serve.

The Bible says it pretty well: "But godliness with contentment is a great gain. For we brought nothing into the world, and we can take nothing out of it" (1 Timothy 6:6, NIV).

Steve speaks internationally more than 200 times yearly at churches, universities, business events, conferences, sales meetings, conventions, and in after dinner formats. To learn more, visit one of his websites: www.SteveDiggs.com; www.NoDebtNoSweat.com; www.RetooledAndRefueled.com. For video and articles go to www.YouTube.com or www.Crosswalk.com and search "Steve Diggs." Call Kyle Froman at 615-403-3805 or 615-300-8263 for scheduling information.